ISSUE NO. 3
2023

A Publication of the SABR Baseball Arts Committee

TURNSTYLE is a publication of the SABR Baseball and the Arts Research Committee. SABR members wishing to submit to the next issue may email turnstyle@sabr.org. Turnstyle accepts creative and literary works including poetry, fiction, cartoons, artwork, and creative nonfiction. Submissions over 250 words should be emailed as attached MS Word Documents. Shorter works may be included in the body of the email. Include an author bio of 50-100 words with submission and your mailing address. No reprints: original/unpublished work only. Turnstyle does not pay for submissions but does provide digital contributor copies and one print copy. Contributors must be members of SABR.

Not a member of SABR? The Society for American Baseball Research exists to stimulate, facilitate, and promulgate research into the game of baseball for purposes of increasing understanding of the game itself and its importance. Anyone with an interest in supporting this mission, whether as a researcher or just an enthusiast for the game, can join SABR. Visit http://sabr.org/join for more information.

ISBNs 978-1-970159-66-0 paperback/ 978-1-970159-65-3 digital
TURNSTYLE: The SABR Journal of Baseball Arts, Issue No. 3
A publication of the SABR Baseball Arts Committee
Published January 2023

Editors: Joanne Hulbert and Jay Hurd
Design and Production: Cecilia Tan
Layout: Meredith J. Evans
Cover Design & Turnstyle Logo Design: Cecilia Tan
Front Cover: Satchel Paige, Plane, All-Stars - Original Artwork by Margie Lawrence
Back Cover: SABR Night at PNC Park, on June 22, 2018 by Kent Putnam
Frontispiece: Safe at Home by Kurt Robinson

Published by:
Society for American Baseball Research, Inc.
Cronkite School at ASU
555 N. Central Ave. #416
Phoenix, AZ 85004
Phone: (602) 496-1560

Contents

Introduction

The premier issue of the *SABR Review of Books: A Forum of Baseball and Literary Opinion* saw publication in 1986. Contributing to that inaugural issue were some of baseball's most notable writers and SABR members – Roger Kahn, John Thorn, Peter Gammons, Dan Okrent, and Pat Jordan, to name a few.

Among the baseball books on our shelves, and stacked on tables, we found four additional volumes of *The SABR Review*, and copies of other publications, including *The Minneapolis, Spitball, Elysian Fields, Fan,* and independently published collections of poetry, prose, and historical commentary. Each of the these, from the playing fields and the pens, celebrate baseball.

Now, *Turnstyle*, the SABR Journal of Baseball and the Arts continues the tradition of sharing baseball literature, artwork, and imagery. Writers, artists, poets, photographers, and others participate in and reflect on baseball and the arts. The first issue of *Turnstyle* offered elements of baseball literature from the past, seeking to inspire contemporary writers and artists to embrace this tradition. The second issue proved that contemporary writers and artists have indeed been inspired to contribute their works. One year ago, we announced a call for submissions for the third issue: the response has been overwhelming, surpassing the number of submissions received for the first two issues. Perhaps the pandemic with its demands for home quarantine and isolation, and the subsequent grim portent of a postponed baseball season, have encouraged the many contributions.

Although we are unable to include in this issue all work received, we say thank you to those who have shared their work. Some material already submitted will be considered for *Turnstyle 4*. We encourage others to find solace in contemplating baseball and the arts, and to share connections with the Great American Pastime.

Joanne Hulbert and Jay Hurd, Co-Editors

I Remember When: Baseball of Another Era

Norman L. Macht

There are few advantages to growing old, beyond the simple fact of survival. Merchants wave discounts at you, and you become eligible for social security while it's still solvent.

But when we old-timers look back, we realize we have something nobody under, say, 70 or so will ever experience: the thrills and excitement, the fascination and fun of growing up in the 1930s and '40s, when baseball was America's domestic form of warfare and not show business. When guys with names like Pepper and Pretzels and Piano Legs and Fats and Bobo fought it out with Slick and Hack and Peanuts and Spud. When the average ballplayer was relatively well paid but was still a working stiff who considered himself lucky to be a big league ballplayer, and happily pumped gas or sold insurance in the wintertime to feed his family, because he could play baseball the other half of the year. When the top four teams in each eight-team league shared in the World Series pool, and that extra five hundred bucks for finishing fourth was worth scrapping for to a guy earning $3,000 a year.

Multi-year contracts were rare, and hungry, talented players were plentiful. Every major leaguer knew next year's contract depended on this year's performance, and the minor leagues were loaded with guys coveting a shot at your job.

Those of us who were witnesses to the decade before World War II probably saw more future Hall of Famers in action during that ten-year span than fans in any other decade that followed. We saw the end of the careers of Babe Ruth, Lou Gehrig, Lefty Grove, Jimmie Foxx and Bill Terry, and the start of those of Joe DiMaggio, Bob Feller, Ted Williams and Hank Greenberg – just names and faces and numbers on cards to today's collectors but living memories to us fortunate graybeards.

I was triple blessed, growing up in the New York City area, where we had the batting averages and personal tics and habits of the Giants, Yankees and Dodgers to memorize. And if you think there's hatred in the Middle East, you should have been a Giants fan in Brooklyn or a Dodger rooter at the Polo Grounds when those teams clashed in the traditional Memorial Day, July 4th and Labor Day doubleheaders. Not since Athens and Sparta fought it out a few millennia ago has there been such a venomous tale of two cities. We have not seen its like since both those teams died and went to heaven or hell – take your

2

choice.

One day Giants' left fielder Joe Moore's brother-in-law, visiting from Texas, went to a doubleheader at Ebbets Field. When he got back home he said, "If you want to go somewhere to see some action, just go up there to see a ball game. I saw 95 fights and two games, all the same day."

The Giants fought with the Cubs and Pirates, too, and the Gashouse Gang from St. Louis fought with everybody, especially on days when Dizzy Dean pitched. Diz was a friend of the dry cleaners; he loved to send hitters sprawling in the dirt while giving them the horse laugh. In those days umpires had not yet learned how to read pitchers' minds, and the brushback pitch was not considered grounds for banishment, or a breach of etiquette like putting your elbows on the supper table. Nobody charged the mound until somebody had low-bridged five or six in a row; then the brawls broke out.

Baseball in the 1930s was set to music. Dugouts echoed with a raucous cacophony of ribald ridicule from bench jockeys and coaches. Nobody was immune. It was nothing personal; nobody took more raw riding than Babe Ruth, and nobody was more beloved by other players. Personal habits, marital problems, religion, ethnic or regional background, physical traits – all were fair game. Verbal savagery did not begin with Jackie Robinson's arrival on the scene.

The object was to rattle the batter or pitcher to distraction or, even better, to wrath, curbing his effectiveness at the plate or on the mound. Some players ignored it; some turned themselves up a notch when under fire; some were "rabbit ears" who picked up every insult and suffered by it.

There was infield music, too: pepper, jazz, birdsong, whistles, encouraging patter. It's all considered bush or kid stuff by today's corporate robots, but it kept the players a little more alert and on their toes, and it added to the distraction of the batter.

Sometimes the catcher joined the chorus; when Birdie Tebbetts was catching and Dick Bartell was at shortstop for the 1940 Tigers, it sounded like an aviary. And in the days when ballparks were built for humans, it was audible to fans in the dollar seats and bleachers alike.

It's all gone now, extinct as the ten-cent hot dog and the hundred-minute game. Most players now are businessmen concerned with image and marketing. Millionaires do not hurl epithets at each other. Pepper is undignified. The brushback pitch is impolite. Union brothers fraternize.

Most of those warriors of the '30s and '40s are gone now. Some have Alzheimer's and cannot recall when the baseball wars were between teams and not between players and owners. But I do, and other fortunate fogies like me do, and we salute them and thank them for the memories and are glad that we were there.

Painting by David Holden

Keeping Score
Dick Butler

I have fond memories of week-long visits with my grandmother, Evelyn (Jones) Butler, in the summers of 1963 and 1964. It was just the two of us at her home on N. Campbell Avenue in Indianapolis. In 1963, I was eight years old while she was 64.

During those weeks, Grandma Butler would serve dinner on a TV tray in her living room—a forbidden practice at my home. It felt like we were co-conspirators in a revolt against all priggish traditions! On her black-and-white television, we watched Bill Burrud travelogues about safaris in the mysterious jungles of Africa.

Since a movie theater was not far from my grandmother's home, she liked to take me to movies on my summer visits. In 1963, she took me to see PT-109, a movie about John F. Kennedy's service in World War II as an officer commanding a motor torpedo boat in the Pacific theater.

But my most cherished memory came one August afternoon in 1963. She knew I was enamored with baseball, so we drove to a shopping center (malls were not yet in vogue) where players from the Indianapolis Indians minor league baseball team were signing autographs. Three players stood in the corner of a store but to my surprise, few fans were present. I was shy but she coaxed me to approach the three players for their autographs. I had nothing for them to sign so I asked Grandma for a piece of paper which she produced from her purse.

I noticed one player who seemed older than the other two. He had short, blond hair and a slight build. Hesitantly, I asked him for his autograph. Smiling, he signed with alacrity, handing the paper back to me. I mumbled my thanks and returned to Grandma. In the car on the way home, I looked more closely at the scribbled paper. I had the autograph of Herb Score!

In 1955, as a rookie pitcher for the Cleveland Indians, Herb Score led the American League in strikeouts, posting a 16-9 record for the Cleveland Indians and winning the Rookie of the Year Award. The next season, Score won 20 games and repeated as the league leader in strikeouts. On May 7, 1957, his promising career was derailed by a major injury when he was struck in the eye by a line drive off the bat of Yankee infielder Gil McDougald. He struggled over the next six seasons, winning just 19 games over that span.

In 1963, when he signed my autograph, Score was pitching for the Indianapolis Indians, then a minor league affiliate of the Chicago White Sox, seeking to revive his flagging career and return to the major leagues. Sadly, Score went 0-6 with a 7.66 ERA for the Indians that year, concluding his pitching career at the age of thirty.

When he signed his autograph for me near the end of his dreadful 1963 season, he must have known he was finished as a pitcher. Yet he waited patiently with other minor leaguers at a nearly empty store in Indianapolis to sign autographs for a few young fans, including a reticent eight-year-old. It was not until years later that I understood what it meant for Herb Score to stand as a professional to the end, even though his career was fading away like a home run ball soaring into the night sky.

It was also not until I grew into adulthood that I understood the love of my grandmother that day—taking me to the shopping center for an autograph of a fading pitcher for the Indianapolis Indians. I am confident my grandmother did not know of Herb Score's Rookie of the Year Award in 1955 or his 20 wins in 1956. I doubt she knew of his pitching struggles following a devastating injury or that he was nearly washed up with the Indianapolis Indians in 1963. But she knew I loved baseball—and that was enough for her to give me a wondrous memory.

The Greatest Reds Fan of All Time

Dick Butler

My great-great-aunt, Nell (Corbly) Watkins, sister of my great-grandmother Clara (Corbly) McIntyre, was a devoted fan of the Cincinnati Reds baseball team. After her husband died of influenza in 1918, she attended many Reds games at Crosley Field, often riding the bus alone to the ballpark. After the Reds installed lights at Crosley in 1935, she even attended some night games by herself--a courageous undertaking for a woman in those times.

We did not see Aunt Nell very often. I recall just one visit to her Cincinnati home sometime around 1963 when I was eight years old and she was nearing 80. She was heavy-set and wore thick, rubber-soled shoes.

Knowing that I was a baseball fan, she lumbered to her bedroom during our visit, returning with a baseball card of Johnny Temple, the second baseman for the Reds in the 1950s. Temple was not Willie Mays or Mickey Mantle, but I had never received a baseball card as a gift before—and certainly not one from a matronly relative. I was stunned by her thoughtfulness.

Taking the card home, I would occasionally pull it out of my box of baseball cards, carefully holding it on the sides with my thumb and forefinger so as not smudge it, turning it over and over, while parsing Temple's career statistics on the back of the card. Temple hit over .300 three times, played on six All-Star teams, and led the National League in walks in 1957.

As an eight-year-old, the card made me realize, for the first time, that superstars like Mantle and Mays were not the only ballplayers worthy of admiration--there were many others like Johnny Temple whose adroit play and dependability commanded my respect. From this, I began to respect ballplayers, and others in all walks of life, who toiled in relative anonymity—quotidian heroes for whom productive work was an intrinsic reward. For years after, I cherished the card as if it were one of the stone tablets of Moses.

After Aunt Nell died in 1975, my mother had a striking dream in which Nell was selected as the greatest Reds fan of all time. The team held a rousing parade through downtown Cincinnati in her honor. Perched atop the cherry red convertible leading the procession, she smiled and waved to a rapturous crowd as confetti fell upon her gray hair and shoulders.

This is all my mother saw in her dream, but it is not difficult to imagine a young boy standing on the sidewalk, cheering for Aunt Nell as she passed by in her mystical time of glory—and waving a Johnny Temple baseball card.

Painting by David Holden

The Game

Richard M. Campbell, Jr.

Lucinda belts Car Wheels on a Gravel Road
As I park on the gravel
Minor league parks, each a little gem
This one no different, as I visit again
I know none of the players, which is OK
I just love to be where baseball is played
The rhythm of the game is familiar
Like a favorite old tune
Heard thousands of times
Yet still fresh and new
As I pull out my wallet to get in the door
It feels likely I will see something that I never have before
With that anticipation I look for my seat
I find it, sit down and place my beer at my feet
Other fans settle in as 80's tunes blare
Some families, young adults, lots of gray hair
I've been here before, I'll be here again
Time for another baseball game to begin

The Dream

Richard M. Campbell, Jr.

Maybe all I need is a shot in the arm
Maybe all I need is a shot in the arm
Maybe all I need is a shot in the arm
The haunting, rhythmic lyrics of Wilco's anthem bounce around in
my mind
As I wake from the dream
It is a new dream, one I have never had
The lyrics take me back to tailgating
A simpler time when "shot in the arm" was a guessing game
About which MLB players used PED's
Maybe all I need is a shot in the arm
Maybe all I need is a shot in the arm
Maybe all I need is a shot in the arm
The new dream is about vaccinating
The new dream is about the Oakland Coliseum
The new dream is about a return to watching live baseball
The new dream is about a picture of myself getting the shot in the
arm
The new dream is about posting that picture on Instagram
The new dream is about hope
Maybe all I need is a shot in the arm
Maybe all I need is a shot in the arm
Maybe all I need is a shot in the arm

Baseball

Kalwinder Singh Dhindsa

"I've always loved baseball. It has always been the case.
Long before I knew what the game was or how it was even played.
Baseball was magic and The Baseball Ground was where you would find it."

I was born in Derby on the 13th of September 1979 and subsequently raised and brought up on Portland Street in the inner city suburb of Pear Tree. For many years in the heart of this community stood The Baseball Ground. A magical place that always enchanted me.

This year, 2020 celebrates the 125th anniversary of Derby County Football Club's first fixture as permanent tenants at The Baseball Ground.

In 1895 it became the home of Derby County Football Club and was used as a professional association football stadium for 102 years until 1997. Eventually its doors were closed, and it was finally demolished in 2003 after 113 years of continuous use. It was a football stadium for 108 years.

However, prior to this The Baseball Ground was used for baseball and was the original home of Derby Baseball Club.

The Baseball Ground.

Kalwinder Singh Dhindsa

Home of Derby County Baseball Club from 1890 to 98.
Three times British Champions. The Baseball diamond. Originate.

Baseball. Introduced by 1st Baronet, Sir Francis Ley.
Founder of Malleable Castings. The Vulcan Ironworks - Derby.

Following a visit to the USA in 1889.
Ley built a ground for the use of his workers to shine.

A young boy born in Cradley a 'striker' at the iron foundry.
A legend that grew to become the destroying angel of Pear Tree.

Playing Baseball and Cricket with bats he would wield.
Steve Bloomer a superstar in every sporting field.

These days more synonymous as a football goalscoring great.
The sinewed steel striker left his mark on home plate.

G is for Ground.

The Baseball to be clear.

Its mud world renowned.

A unique unrelenting

atmosphere.

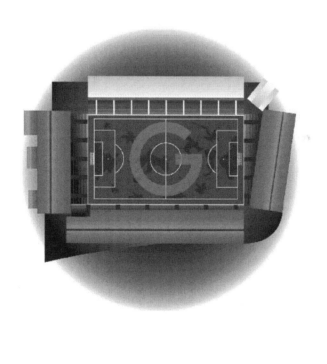

"If you build it, he will come."

I was 10 years old when I first heard the voice in the film 'Field of Dreams' based on the book *Shoeless Joe* by W. P. Kinsella. Thirty years later that voice remains a driving force in my life.

A couple of years previously I had first come across the name of the legendary Steve Bloomer when I stumbled across a plaque as I was walking past the stadium. Ever since then Steve Bloomer and The Baseball Ground have become synonymous with happiness for me.

Most people who know anything about Football will know that Steve Bloomer was one of the earliest superstars of the game, but not many people will know that he also played baseball. It was at Derby where he became a three time National Baseball Champion with the Derby Baseball Club.

He/Art

Kalwinder Singh Dhindsa

Impossible dreams he did evoke,

Andy Edwards the man from Stoke.

Get down here fast and leave your mark.

Steve Bloomer's watching at Pride Park.

Derby County's revered icons.

Sculpt in clay and cast in bronze.

The boy from Pear Tree he did take part.
Your broken heart he turned to art.

On March 1, 2006 I lost my father to suicide. I was heartbroken and my world was turned upside down. For a long time after I found myself in a very dark and unhappy place in my life. But the one thing that would always raise my spirits was thinking back to my childhood and happier days in Pear Tree.

Over the next few years, I began writing more and more about my life and the people within it. Steve Bloomer and The Baseball Ground played a monumental role during my growth, decay and transformation. So, I naturally returned to the old baseball ground at the end of my story *My Father & The Lost Legend of Pear Tree*.

Are we dreaming?

Kalwinder Singh Dhindsa

'Wake up Kal, he's here', the voice of football whispered into my ear.
'Who's here?', I asked.
'And what is John Motson doing in my bed', I thought to myself.

I was now sat up in my bed, fully clothed. I felt something close to my heart. I reached for it and then pulled it out of my breast pocket. It was a coin. It was Gian Singh's coin. The same coin he had given to me in Sahabpur. I put it back in my pocket and then looked around in the darkness.

The front door blew wide open as a gust of wind rushed into the house, followed by the sound of thousands of cheering fans. I hadn't heard those cheers in years, especially in Pear Tree. They seemed to be coming from the direction of the old Baseball Ground.

'Go home Kal', said the voice of football.

'But I am home', I replied.

In the very next second, I found myself strangely floating out of my bed and then down the stairs and out through the open front door into the night. My feet did not even touch the ground as I was slowly carried away from my house on the hill, towards a light through the darkness.

In the near distance I saw the backs of hundreds of marching Sherwood Foresters who had streamed out from the old Normanton Barracks. As I followed them towards the light the sound of the cheers became louder and louder the closer I was carried to the source. A shining bright light now lit up a path to the old ballpark followed by the sound of marching feet.

'Come on Kal, he's waiting, follow me', beckoned a black silhouette of a man.

A presence continued to carry me forward closely following the shadow ahead. We passed the nursery, the old Pear Tree schools, the Wallis clothing factory and then down towards the field. In no time at all we had arrived at Shaftesbury Crescent.

As we approached the Baseball Ground entrance the intense bright light of the Sunday morning sunrise began to consume the black silhouette of a man ahead of me.

I stopped at the entrance, where I had first seen Bloomer's tablet all those

B is for Bloomer.

Steve of Pear Tree.

The legendary footballer.

Who was born in Cradley.

years ago, but it was not there and as soon as I realised this, the cheers evaporated into the night. A cuc-coo, coo pierced the silence.

Suddenly a shower-room door appeared from out of the old brickwork.

'Tokens please', a voice from the other side called out.

'But I don't have one', I replied as my feet softly touched down on the earth below.

'You sure kid? Come on now. Hand it over'.

I looked down at my hand and in my palm I was holding Gian Singh's coin again. I inspected it carefully. A Pear Tree on one side and a sideward profile of a face on the other. The word Ruhleben written above his head with the roman numerals 28 and 23 on either side. 1874 and Dum Spiro Spero written below. The man on the coin then turned his head towards me and winked. There was no doubt about it. The watcher had been silently observing me all along.

The coin in my hand began to glow with a golden hue and then looking up I noticed that a slot had appeared in the shower room door. It was obviously a sign. So, I inserted the coin into the hole. The shower room door vanished and from behind it appeared a man with a lovely flapping moustache.

'Follow me kid, we've been expecting you. My name's Hudson. All the birds call me Chaz. You can call me Charles'.

I was led onto the Baseball Ground pitch, but it was not the field I expected. Yes, it was covered in luscious green grass, but it was not a football field, rectangular in shape, it was instead, a baseball diamond.

'Mr Kinsella has done a great job laying it out for us all to play ball on', said Charles.

'Wondrous Perfection', I replied, what a pretty park.

I began walking towards the pitcher's mound.

'He's been waiting for you', said a voice from behind me.

I looked back to see where it had come from. There was no one in sight but my shadow beneath me.

'Go on Kal'. I looked back down at my feet again and then noticed that my shadow had disappeared, even though the light still shone bright.

I looked up and a white silhouette of a man appeared in front of me. A face then emerged out of it. I recognised him immediately. It was Ben Warren. He had stepped out of the darkness and into the light. He looked happy, he smiled.

'He's been wanting to meet you for years ... we all have', said Ben.

'Who Ben? Who?', I replied.

Ben stepped aside and, in the distance,, leaning against a brick wall, with his back to me, I saw him. 'It can't be ...?', I whispered to myself. The man against the brick wall began to slowly turn his body and face towards me. I stood in awe, fixed to the spot. On seeing me he winked and nodded in acknowledgement. 'DERBY', blazoned across the chest of his pin stripe black and white baseball jersey.

'My Goodness. It was him', I heard myself say in disbelief.

Steve Bloomer had returned home just like the indomitable King of Rome.

I took a deep breath and grabbed the lapels of my jacket as I walked towards him. My saviour, the destroying angel now stood a few feet away, staring right back at me.

'I never forgot you Steve', I said to him.

He smiled and then grasped my hand with a firm handshake.

I smiled in relief, 'Thanks for always being there Steve'.

'No Kal. Thank you. You never gave up', replied Bloomer.

My eyes welled with tears, so I momentarily looked away but as I did so I noticed a sign above the coach's box. 'The Derby County Baseball Club'.

I looked back at Bloomer, intrigued. He then pointed towards the stadium tannoy.

'STEPHEN BLOOMER', called out the voice of football.

'BRIAN HOWARD CLOUGH'

'PETER THOMAS TAYLOR'

'DAVID CRAIG MACKAY'

'HUGH KILPATRICK GALLACHER'

'JOHN DAVID STAMPS'

'JOHN KIRBY'

'ALICE ANN WHEELDON'

'STEPHEN HENRY WETTON'

Mr. Wetton?!?! I said in astonishment. 'How's he made your team?'

Bloomer looked at me, surprised.

'Did he not tell you? He played for Derby County F.C. He was a Derby Boy', said Bloomer.

'Well, he did, but we all thought he was pulling our leg', I replied.

'Good old Wetton. He loves telling stories. Never stops talking that one. Harry Storer recommended him to us, said he was a good catch. Young Steve has a good heart and always keeps our spirits high', said Bloomer.

I could not believe what I was hearing, I listened on in bewilderment, unsure whether Bloomer was being serious or not. 'He also wrote Growing Pains for the BBC you know?' At this point I burst out into a fit of laughter as I noticed Bloomer grinning at me.

Only when the last of my chuckles subsided did I then say to him in all seriousness, 'But Mr Wetton's not dead. What's he doing here?'.

'Everyone is welcome. No one is dead here, Kal. No one truly dies when their name is still spoken. Nobody dies in dreamland. Everybody lives.'

I began to choke up. 'Hey Steve, is this Heaven?', I asked.

Bloomer looked straight through me with his piercing grey eyes. The hairs on the back of my neck now stood to attention as a spark of electricity charged through my spine and out through my crown. I felt a hand on my shoulder from behind me, its fingers brushed my face.

'No son, it's Pear Tree. Thanks for looking after my boy, Steve,' said my father.

'Kal Singh Dhindsa is our friend, Mohinder,' Bloomer replied.

My father looked down at me, smiled and then bit his bottom lip.

'It's good to see you again Kally,' he said as he hugged me.

'I missed you so much, Dad. I'm sorry I couldn't be there for you when you needed me', I said as I wept into his chest.

'It's ok, son. Don't worry. It's ok. I'm here. I never left you. Everything will be ok from now on,'he said.

My father then pulled out a baseball from his parka pocket and placed it in my hand. 'I think you owe Steve this pitch,'

I was overcome with emotion and filled with pride. Steve Bloomer had brought my father home to me. 'Hey Steve! heads-up,' I called out as I turned quickly on my heel and threw the baseball as hard as I could in his direction.

Steve Bloomer smashed it out of the ballpark.

He always did.

*

A saucepan boiled over in the distance.

'Mum must have the tea on, Dad?'

'Let's go home son, we'll pick some milk up on the way back. She'll be waiting for us.'

Honu$

Kalwinder Singh Dhindsa

One of the greatest baseball players that ever existed,
The Honus Wagner baseball card elegantly depicted.
Designed and issued by the American Tobacco Company,
Between 1909 to 11 as part of its T206 Series ATC.
But Wagner refused to allow the production to continue,
Either not wanting children to buy cigarettes, or more money want-
ed owed to.
The ATC thus stopped producing the card attributed.
With a total of only 50 to 200 ever publicly distributed.
It now ranks as the most coveted baseball card of all time.
One recently having sold for over 30,000,000 dime.

22

Casey Struck Out Again

John Jakicic

Somewhere bands are still playing while hearts remain light
Somewhere men are still laughing while kids shout with glee
But still no joy in Mudville since all of us think
Mudville hasn't been "somewhere" since Casey's strike three

But there's more to the story of Casey's at-bat
Which begins with strike three — then the bulletin came
To announce that the teams would return to the field
Because late-breaking news said we still had a game

Seems an umpire called a timeout in advance
Of the pitcher beginning his pitch to the plate
Therefore, Casey was handed a huge second chance
When his lucky stars pulled off this great twist of fate

Still with Jimmy on second and Flynn hugging third
And the score 4 to 2 with just one out to go
Mighty Casey returned to the plate 0-and-2
And again doffed his hat as the cheers start to grow

Then he crushed the first pitch over five hundred feet
Barely fair, but called foul, yet he wasn't deterred
Till a manager held up four fingers to show
That a strategy shift was about to occur

Once the catcher stood straight with his right arm outstretched
Casey swore to high heaven he's madder than hell
Then he cursed out the skipper who ordered his walk
While he flipped him the finger which works just as well

But ball one caught his eye cuz it wasn't that wide
And when ball two inched closer as well as ball three
Casey's ready to pounce on ball four though he knew

That some luck from his stars once again would be key

Then when ball four was luckily lobbed within reach
Casey ripped it to right as a low, line-drive shot
While the right fielder stretched for a tough shoestring catch
As it quickly sinks in — he just screwed up a lot

When he let the ball roll to the right-field wall
Letting Jimmy and Flynn tie the game at all four
And as Casey rounds second, he knows he'll make third
But there's five thousand Mudville fans screaming for more

So he thundered past third but was running on fumes
And away from his coach who kept hollering "Stop!"
Of course, Casey looked back and yelled "Shut the hell up!"
As he blew through a stop sign proceeding nonstop

Meanwhile, both relay throws wound up hitting their mark
And the last one beat Casey without any doubt
Who was huffing and puffing but simply could not
Put the pedal to metal just plumb tuckered out

But he found a new gear when approaching home plate
Where a catcher just sits with a ball in his mitt
Who's awaiting his obvious, upcoming fate
Lying flat on his back from a bone-crushing hit

As the bodies collided, suspense filled the air
Plus two caps and a mask though too early to call
But once Casey touched home plate by then the ump knew
That a mitt tagged him first — then the mitt dropped the ball

And so Mudville is "somewhere" still basking in joy
And what's more, Ernest Thayer would surely agree
That we all will remember and never forget
Mighty Casey struck out — all our thoughts of strike three

To Ron Cey

Joey Nicoletti

Mr. Cey, you captured my imagination
when I learned your nickname:

Penguin, like Batman's enemy.
You were also a reviled supervillain:

your perfect blond hair and moustache
made my mother believe and say

that Robert Redford looked like you.
This made veins bulge from my father's

sweaty neck like dead redwood roots,
almost as much as the frozen ropes

and round-trippers you smacked
against the Yankees every October—

the red face of the leather-lunged sun,
shouting across the dirty dusk horizon.

To Jimmie Crutchfield

Joey Nicoletti

(1910—1993)

Dear Mr. Crutchfield:
I never saw you
catch fly balls barehanded.
I never saw you
steal bases or stretch
singles into doubles or triples.
But tonight, when I see

Comet Neowise
zoom past moons and planets,
I imagine you, running
the bases in Greenlee Field;
stars foaming
in a clear Pittsburgh sky
like a radiant round of beers.

To Gene Richards

Joey Nicoletti

Dear Mr. Richards,
I learned how to choke up
on the bat
by watching you on TV.
So when I tried it in
a little league game,
I got my first hit of the season,
a ground ball with eyes,
which I tried to stretch
into a double by running
as fast as I could, like you did,
which might have worked if
I had your speed and baserunning acumen,
and if the burly left fielder didn't
gun me down
like a shabby outlaw
in a spaghetti western
before the credits fell
in the darkness
like too many stars
to wish upon.

Sparkling Memories From a Dreary Day

Francis Kinlaw

Since June of 1953, I have recalled again and again events that occurred when I witnessed my first two major-league baseball games in the company of my father. Stories linking fathers and sons and baseball are common in literature and folklore, but my personal experience carries a significance that has always been very special to me in light of an unfortunate event that occurred less than four months later. My father would die suddenly of a stroke at the age of 51, and I would become fatherless before reaching my ninth birthday. This story, however, is not really about baseball or my father's death, and it certainly is not a tale of woe because a dedicated and caring mother managed to guide my three siblings and me through a period of temporary grief and into adulthood. Rather, my story is about memories of a day that would be considered routine under ordinary circumstances but, due to developments that followed, remains indelible in my mind.

First of all, the specific date: June 6, 1953. What was my father thinking during our 40-mile trip into Detroit from our home in Algonac, Michigan? Although it would have been pointless for him to broach the subject in even an elementary manner with me, I must suppose that he was reflecting on events that had occurred on the beaches of France exactly nine years earlier. On the anniversary of D-Day, he was likely thinking---as I have so many times as an adult---how quickly nine years pass into time. And, because I had been born a mere five months after the invasion of Europe, he probably looked at me that day and was amazed that his young son was growing up so quickly!

I, on the other hand, could only attempt to contain my excitement over the prospect of seeing my beloved Detroit Tigers (a truly woeful team that occupied last place in the American League with only 10 victories in its first 44 games) face the visiting Boston Red Sox in a doubleheader. To demonstrate my firm support on the occasion of my first personal encounter with the players, I had worn my favorite Tigers T-shirt and a brand-new Tigers cap.

Despite a steady drizzle that had been falling from dark gray skies since early morning, I don't believe that I ever considered the possibility that the twin bill might not be played. After all, love is supposedly blind, and my devotion to the Tigers was complete. I had begun to follow the team on a day-to-day basis in 1951, and baseball became one of my "areas of concentration" during the

28

following season. My mother, a math teacher who placed only faith and family above the value of education, did not object to my growing fascination with the game. My father, an electrician employed by the Detroit Edison Company who followed not only major-league players but also stars of the Negro Leagues such as Satchel Paige, enthusiastically encouraged my interest in the sport.

Prior to this trip to my first game, my insatiable hunger for Tigers baseball had been satisfied by listening to Van Patrick's descriptions of games on the club's radio network and watching the relatively few contests that were televised in the Detroit area. As I listened to or watched games, I had a habit of referring to and even memorizing information about opposing players from the backs of baseball cards sold by the Topps Chewing Gum Company. For example, if Bob Feller were pitching for the Cleveland Indians against the Tigers, I would not only study his image on the card but also every statistic relating to his career. My mother was very pleased with this activity, believing that calculating batting averages, slugging percentages, and earned-run averages fostered mathematical development. I naturally shared her opinion at the time and, as a matter of fact, still do.

Between games, I spent countless hours sitting at our kitchen table with my cherished collection of baseball cards of Tigers players, especially cards which were included in packages of Glendale Meats products prior to and during the 1953 season. The aroma coming from those cards did not dissipate even when the cards were kept in open air for weeks, but the lingering odor of wieners was every bit as appealing to me as the fragrance of a fine perfume would become in later years. Besides, my boyhood heroes such as Jim Delsing, Harvey Kuenn, and Ned Garver surely didn't smell any better than those baseball cards after long games played in the heat of summer!

When my father and I arrived in the vicinity of the ballpark on that Saturday morning, a sense of reality regarding the weather finally registered with me. My father informed me that the first game of the doubleheader had been delayed by the rain and that we would be eating lunch at a small restaurant located near Briggs Stadium. While I am certain that I was disappointed and frustrated, I must have adapted to the situation because I remember having a pleasant conversation with my father at a table in the very crowded and smoky diner. As we ate, my eyes were drawn to a window and the falling rain. In retrospect, I am convinced that had my parents not believed that the weather would improve by early afternoon, the trip into the city would have never occurred. And the weather did indeed improve, although dark clouds remained after the intensity of the rain decreased.

By the time we finished our sandwiches, the rain had turned once again into a drizzle and word circulated in the restaurant that the first game of the twin bill would begin 45 minutes after the announced starting time. Upon receiving that good news, we left the diner and made our way to the ballpark.

Briggs Stadium, which would be renamed Tiger Stadium in 1961, was considered in the 1950s to be one of major-league baseball's best and most attractive venues. And attractive it was! Despite my overwhelming sense of anticipation and imagination of a larger-than-life structure, I had no idea that my first view of a major-league field would be so incredibly magical and awe-inspiring! Upon entering the stadium, my eyes nearly popped out of my head as I observed a broad expanse of rich green turf entirely surrounded by a double-decked stadium with more than 53,000 seats that had been painted as green as the grass. An immense scoreboard towered over the upper-deck bleacher seats in center field, and tall light towers had been installed at various points around the stadium. I now realize that those dark clouds which irritated me so much that day did provide one worthwhile bonus: their presence ensured that, with radiant light projected from the towers, I would have an opportunity to absorb the atmosphere of a night game in the middle of an afternoon.

My dad and I immediately went to our seats in the lower deck between home plate and third base, close to the Tigers' dugout but too far away to make eye contact with or converse with any of the players. I was very content--- thrilled, in fact---to watch players from both teams warm up in preparation for the game and to see in living color the Tigers' home white uniforms with a distinctive royal "D" on the left side of the chest, their dark blue hats also featuring the royal "D," and dark blue stockings with horizontal orange stripes. The Boston uniforms were also colorful, basic gray with blue-and-red trim.

To my young eyes, the crowd seemed huge even in the massive stadium. The perceptions of this eight-year-old boy were, however, inaccurate to say the least. Researching the game years later to confirm or correct my original impressions of the day, I was shocked to learn that the combination of undesirable weather conditions and the Tigers' poor level of performance had resulted in a paid attendance of only 6,957. To me, the crowd had seemed to number no less than 50,000!

Once the first game of the doubleheader actually began, I took in my surroundings and thoroughly enjoyed talking to my father about plays and individual players. All these years later, I remember only one specific play that can be found in record books: a leaping catch by Red Sox centerfielder Hoot Evers near the outfield fence. The Red Sox won the first game by a score of 6-2 behind the pitching of Willard Nixon and then posted a narrow victory in the nightcap as lefthander Mel Parnell hurled a 1-0 shutout. I was disappointed that the only home run of the day came off the bat of Boston's Sammy White, while my father was likely surprised that the Tigers' ineffective pitching staff did not surrender at least three or four long blasts.

One incident that occurred on the field that afternoon has remained in my mind. Early in the first game, a ball ricocheted loudly off of home-plate umpire Jim Duffy's inflated chest protector (umpires held large protectors in front of their bodies in those days) and, as would be expected, the spectators erupted in good-natured cheering. My father laughed out loud, and the sound of his laugh was wonderful. Taking my cue, I laughed with him.

We watched all of the first game and approximately five innings of the second, but then my father gently explained that we needed to leave and begin our trip back to Algonac. I would return to Briggs Stadium on August 19, 1953 with my Little-League team to see the Tigers take on the Cleveland Indians. The Tigers won that game, 4-2, and when I got home, I told my father all about how "our team" had defeated future Hall-of-Fame pitcher Early Wynn. I had wished he had been there with me---most especially when I temporarily became sepa-rated from my friends and went into an absolute panic!

One month after that, my father died.

A single afternoon…Shared time together in a cozy restaurant in the middle of a big city…Time spent together on the rides to and from the ball-park…Communication between a father and son in a beautiful place, with no sense by either of us that our time together was dwindling.

I have had many decades to think about that afternoon and all that it meant to me at the time and has since. Its significance to me is obvious, but reflection has led me to understand a fact that is even more important and ultimately more valuable than the particular events of that special day. And who would have ever thought that, of all things, the rain that threatened for hours to dampen my hopes would turn out to be a symbolic component in a valuable lesson for life!

But the moral of my story is true…RAINY DAYS ARE SOMETIMES THE VERY BEST DAYS OF ALL.

THE MARCH OF TIME

Francis Kinlaw

Baseball hopes ride high in each gentle spring breeze,
Crucial plays occur in hot summer months;
Pennant races end as leaves fall from trees,
Winter reflection replaces homers and bunts.

Like seasons and events, careers also evolve,
As temperatures change, players' fates rise and fall;
In time fame will fade and skills will dissolve,
Life's clock moves fast though humans wish it would crawl.

Young phenoms attract with throws and long swats,
Until their arms, legs or instincts decline;
Then as grizzled veterans they pray to hold roster spots
And to retain a place "on the pine."

The Magnetism of the Baseball Cap

John L. Green

Nature was in a pleasant mood, as the blue sky and bright sun joined with the cool crisp air and made this a perfect day for Linda and me to explore Mount Rainier. Mid-September is a beautiful time of year to visit this park, the day about equidistant between summer heat, as far as Washington has heat, and the severe cold being delivered soon by fall and winter.

The day had already been spectacular for us. A home cooked breakfast in the campground filled our energy tanks before we started the 40-mile drive to Mt. Rainier National Park. As we approached a bridge over a small creek, we both began to smile ear-to-ear which quickly advanced to giggling and further moved to all-out cracking up! It ended as suddenly as it began. We looked at the other and wondered what had caused this eruption of happy noise. Were we losing it? Were we characters in a Stephen King novel? Then a sign told us we had just crossed over Laughingwater Creek! Amazing!

Throughout the drive in the park, the glacier-covered peak was with us, alternately disappearing then reappearing as the road turned.

At the Paradise Inn we stopped for lunch, and we walked around this wonderful lodge, still containing original wooden tables and seating in the main hall. The inn will closeout its 83rd year in a couple of weeks for the winter. From this point we hiked the Nisqually Vista Trail. We meandered through colorful flowered meadows. At a trio of overlooks, we viewed the largest glacier on the mountain, the Nisqually Glacier. We could make out the coloring and crevasses on it and watched the tumbling streams of water running down its steep slopes, the water milky gray from glacier flour. Throughout the day we were in dense forests, different than other western forest areas because of the extensive ground plants and ferns. A thick carpet of moist needles cushioned each step as we walked among the tall trees.

Back at the inn, Linda offered to be the runner for ice cream cones while I looked for a place to sit. A clear view of the mountain summit reminded me of how our lands are so beautiful, and our good fortune as we enjoy these scenes. As I made my way to a rock ledge that I intended would be my hard resting place, I noticed the fella with whom I would share this ledge. His baseball cap was the first thing I noticed, a Seattle Mariners' cap, dark blue with the bright blue-green bill and the familiar large "S" overlaying the compass points. I asked, "Hi, you a

Mariners' fan?" The contrast is so pronounced: in crowded cities, people pass one another, scurrying from one point to another, not looking at others, not speaking to others, suspicious of others. But place those same people among God's natural wonders, and people become friendly, considerate, curious, wanting to know the stories of strangers.

Mike was about 75-80 years old who, with his granddaughter and her two pre-teen daughters, had driven from their home in Chehalis, about 70 miles west of the park. Holding his own ice cream cone, he returned the greeting with a "Hello, yes I am!" He responded to my question and gave me background for his being in this spot. I noticed him to be on the slender side, but not frail. He was dressed in tan, trousers, shirt, and even the windbreaker—all tan. His shoes matched his outfit, unpolished brown dress shoes, which surprised me. I wondered why men of this age often extract themselves from comfortable tennis shoes; I should have asked him. While listening to Mike, I noticed the skies were still bright blue and the summit was clear.

After his 360-degree lick around his ice cream, he asked about our background. While I told him of our 6-month trip around the country, I sensed he was interested in more, so I went on and described the route and a few of the highlights. Still interested, Mike asked, "So, you from Cincinnati?" A quick glance down reminded me I was wearing the Cincinnati Reds shirt this day. I replied, "No, but I bought it at Cinergy Field in Cincinnati." Now more than interested, he questioned me, "So, you saw a game there?" I answered, "Yes, we picked up a shirt in each of the baseball parks this season." Mike's eyes seemed to get larger as he asked, "How many parks did you go to?" "All," I replied, at which point I thought I detected the years rolling back in Mike's life, almost like a slot machine's spinning wheels. Soon it came to be that Mike's right eye seemed to have registered "19", and the left, "45"—"1945."

Linda appeared with our cones, just as Mike was crunching on the last of his, but I believed he was not aware of the taste as his mind was taking him back to 1945. He went on to tell us, "During the last year of the war, I was a patient in Letterman Army Hospital at the San Francisco Presidio." I failed to ask him the reason for his hospitalization, and he did not go into it. He continued, "I loved baseball, ever since I was a young boy. As you know, the San Francisco Seals had a good team in the Pacific Coast League, and I would follow them in the newspapers." Now with a slight devilish look in his eye, he said, "Well, once I was on the mend, some of the nurses would turn a blind eye when the Seals were in town. I would check-out a bicycle, take the long, hilly ride over to Seals' Stadium, and catch a game." Mike closed by offering, "When I was a boy, growing up in Chicago, Augie Galan was my favorite player, although he didn't play for the Seals that year in San Francisco." I was convinced this was a true story and not runaway imagination as I was aware Augie Galan was a player of note in both the Pacific Coast League and the majors, playing outfield for the Cubs and Dodgers in the 30s and 40s.

As if on cue, Mike's family appeared, and he introduced us, telling his relatives of our trip. We talked a few more minutes before we wished each other well, and we expressed our happiness that we had met.

As Linda and I walked to the van, we looked up to see the sun and the snow as they joined forces and gave birth on the summit. We watched condensation build to a small cloud, and, when large enough, the cloud was gently released to lazily float east from the mountain just as another was developing.

We had so many similar-type experiences during the trip. There are not too many topics that can get memories flowing out of people, but "baseball" is one, and we were glad we had met Mike of Chehalis, Washington. These unexpected jewels, the stories of those we met along the way made the trip even more exciting, and we looked forward to the next chance meeting.

Patriotic and Grandfatherly Pride

John L. Green

The phone rang just as they were hurrying to leave the house on their way to separate destinations. Linda was upstairs blow-drying her hair, moving quickly to avoid running late. She had offered to manage the visual and audio portion of a Memorial Service for a long-time church member, a man of advanced age who had recently passed away. Linda had committed to this service, but each was disappointed they would not be together this afternoon of a hot August day in 2011.

Moving at warp speed, John was putting on shorts and a baseball tee-shirt. His destination was a different type of celebration than Linda's, not a celebration of a life, but a celebration of a game. He was going to a baseball game, a Little League game being played at Los Cerros Middle School in Danville, just a few miles from home. He couldn't contain his excitement as Linda and John's grandson, Tyler, was the starting pitcher for this monumental game. The winner of this game would be playing in the Northern California Championship Game, one game of many being played around the nation and the world that would eventually determine the two teams that would face-off in the Little League World Series championship game. Today's game time was 1:00 p.m., and it was already 12:15 when the telephone rang.

"Hey, Bubba," Traci began. It is an unusual greeting from one's daughter. Traci was the source of John's oft used nickname, going back to the early 80s. At that time John was wearing a pair of golden shorts when he came down the stairs one hot summer day. Traci, upon looking at him and his attire, shouted to the family, "Hey, look, here comes Bubba Whitelegs!" It stuck.

"You gonna make it in time?" she asked.

"Yes, I'm on my way in one minute," he responded.

"There's a problem here," she continued. After his murmur to go on, Traci said, "There is no one to sing the National Anthem. Do you think you would sing it?"

Without hesitation, John replied, "Sure."

With new excitement in her voice, Traci told him, "Great! I'll tell the Little League rep. Can you be here by 12:45?"

He answered, "I'll leave in two minutes and be there on time."

John double-timed upstairs to tell Linda of this new development. She told him, "You'll do fine. Wish I could be there," as he bounded back down the stairs.

Just as he grabbed his cap, and opened the door, the phone rang once again. He thought of letting Linda pick it up, but decided she had enough going on, so he answered and heard Traci once again, "Bad news, they don't have the background recording. You will have to sing it without instrumental music. Can you still sing it?"

"Sure, that's even better!" he replied, and then he started questioning himself. Why did he think it was better without the music? But there was no time to consider it further, it was done, and he hit the door running.

As he turned the ignition in the camper van, his thoughts turned to the lyrics of the National Anthem. Although certain the words were ingrained in his 70-year-old brain, John still took the opportunity to sing the anthem aloud as he drove to the game. After about four repeats, he proclaimed to himself, "Yes, no problemo!" But as often happens, the lyrics continued to play within his mind, accompanying any other actions and thoughts that came up.

During the drive, he discovered why he was OK, not uncomfortable without music accompaniment. He, like no doubt many of his age, tires, almost grinds his teeth and tightens his jaw when hearing the National Anthem performed by some celebrity or another. It's got to the point he mutes the TV once he hears the first couple of words if they cause elevated blood pressure. The celebrity invariably performs the anthem as if the experience is solely about them. John suspects in their mind, the nation takes a back seat to the performance. Then the warbling begins, notes thrown all over the place, no-where near how it was written. John often wonders if the performer is aware of the significance of the lyrics, aware of when it was written, aware of the atmosphere that existed when written, even aware of the author. To John, it is a sad situation. But then he wonders if his are the musings of an old man, believing that everything before was better than today.

This was the key to his comfort-level, he would sing without accompaniment. He would not have to compete with the musical instruments that might be too loud or the tempo, too slow or too fast. He would sing it as written, pause just an instant after each phrase to underscore the significance, and clearly enunciate each word.

John stood at home plate, the Little League representative stood next to him, holding the microphone. She asked all the players and coaches to line-up in the infield, one team along the 3rd base line, the other along the 1st base line, just like in World Series pre-game announcements. In unison they recited the Little League Pledge and affirmed their commitment by reciting:

> I trust in God
> I love my country
> And will respect its laws
> I will play fair
> And strive to win
> But win or lose
> I will always do my best.

The representative requested all players and fans to stand and remove their caps. She asked all to look to the flagpole, in the left field corner, where Old Glory ruffled in the slight breeze, flying atop our California State Flag. Then she announced to all, "Singing our National Anthem today will be John Green, the Grandfather of San Ramon player, Tyler Coulson."

John was prepared, although there was a slight weakness to his legs at the beginning. It came out as he hoped it would, he performed it with reverence and respect for our nation. All was quiet until he finished; no one in the crowd of 100 or so, roared towards the end as is often done at large stadiums. There must have been many of John's age in the crowd, others who had strong beliefs as to how this national treasure should be performed. Many applauded the rendition, and John felt honored. But his best moment came immediately after singing the anthem. As the players ran to their respective dugouts, Tyler altered his course and made a b-line to John. This handsome, thoughtful 10-year-old boy hugged John around the waist, looked up at John, and said, "I love you, Papa." John's heart almost burst with love for this young boy, with love for this nation.

Later Tyler told John that while the singing was going on, a couple of his teammates, standing near him, whispered, "Tyler, is that really your Grandfather?" When Tyler gave them the affirmative, the teammates said, "That is so cool!"

Mystic Transportation with Don Orsillo {09.06.20}

Gabriel Bogart

you know you're a dorky
baseball fan when you have thoughts
such as

most chants are based on
two-or-three-syllabled meters

in between moments
of folding sheets, wrinkled a bit
since they came out of the drier
23 hours ago.

it's been 12.7 seconds
since I last read a baseball tweet

the entirety of my tiny apartment
smells like magic honey-infused
homemade BBQ sauce from
two nights ago.

the buttery smooth baritone
of play-by-play maestro Don Orsillo
is a soothing balm
against a crushing world.

I can shift into
mystic transportation
when Don's voice forms the phonemes
"welcome to Slam Diego!"

a well-adhered quarantine life
is much like a physics thought experiment:

I am Schrödinger's Cat, but
hearing the world outside the box
codes me as just barely more
alive than dead;
the way I exhale after a close
unassisted double-play at second.

how can I trade for Fernando Tatís, Jr.
in my fantasy league?
I nearly shed a tear of joy
watching him crush that 86 mph cutter
from Yusmeiro Petit

Tatís off of Petit
has a quizzical phonetic symmetry.

I use the commercial break
to wage war with a fitted sheet.

The Home of the Braves

Matthew Perry

Robert called Jack and said he wanted to meet him at Durgin-Park, which Jack took as a bad sign. Robert only went there when something was wrong. He went to his favorite bar, Jacob Wirth's, when he wanted to celebrate; every birthday for the last ten years, after the Braves clinched the pennant in 1948, and after the Red Sox lost to the Indians a few days later. Durgin-Park is where he went when things were bad. They said that five years ago, after the Braves lost to the Indians in the '48 World Series, he spent the entire day and most of the night there, and he only left after the waitstaff carried him to State Street and put him in a cab.

Jack was running late, and when he walked up the stairs, he saw Robert sitting at a table by a window chewing on a piece of cornbread. There were a couple of empty glasses on the table, and he was staring out into space, lost in thought. Jack walked over and waved his hand in front of his face.

Robert snapped back to reality.

"Jack! Welcome to my office. Please, have a seat."

He pulled out the chair across from him and sat down. "You okay Bob?" he asked.

Robert didn't respond right away. After a moment he said "Well, to be honest, I've been better. I have some news to share with you…"

He trailed off, staring again at a picture of a lobster on the brick wall. The restaurant was about half full, with a few couples and families dining at the long tables around them. The low hum of people talking was interrupted by clinking glasses and the scratching of chairs on the wood floor. Waitresses walked by with trays of drinks, clam chowder, baked beans, and prime rib.

"What is it? Is it Mary? Did she kick you out?"

Robert's wife Mary was often kicking him out of the house after long nights at bars, road trips where he didn't call enough, and when she thought he was being a little too "friendly" with the players' wives and girlfriends. He would win her back with some flowers or jewelry, and things would be okay until she kicked him out again.

"No, no, Mary is fine, we are doing alright. This is something worse. Much, much worse. You're not going to believe me when I tell you. I'll come out and say it, but you are going to have to brace yourself."

41

Jack grabbed onto his hat in an over-exaggerated manner. Robert was always being dramatic about things and Jack learned that he should take him with a grain of salt.

"I just got news from Quinn that he talked to Perini and they are moving the team."

Jack's hands dropped back down to his sides. "What? Moving the team where? The suburbs?"

Lou Perini was the owner of the Boston Braves and everyone knew he wanted out of Braves Field in Brighton. The stadium was showing its age and there wasn't enough parking. The place sat mostly empty throughout last season and the rumor was he wanted to take the team outside of the city and build a brand-new stadium with ample parking and modern amenities.

"Not quite Framingham, a little further west. They are taking the team to Milwaukee. They are going to be the Milwaukee Braves."

"You've got to be kidding me. This is a joke, right?"

"Dead serious" he said.

Jack was dumbfounded. How could they do this to me he thought. He had only worked for the organization for two years doing promotions and public relations, but he had been a fan for all of his life. To Jack, Boston without the Braves was like Egypt without the Pyramids.

"When did all this happen?" asked Jack.

"The National League owners voted on it earlier today. Perini has been planning it for a long time, but he kept it mostly to himself. They are taking over the minor league stadium and moving out there immediately."

"So, what, they are just up and leaving? Are they taking us with them?"

"Quinn says he's not sure yet. We might be able to move with the team, but I don't know, who wants to live in Milwaukee? I have heard the winters there are brutal."

"It's not like Boston has great winters," Jack said.

"I know, but at least we have the ocean here."

"I've heard Lake Michigan looks like an ocean. There are even beaches there, and lighthouses."

"Hey, whose side are you on?" said Robert, his voice rising. "If you like Milwaukee so much why don't you abandon me too and move there." People at other tables started to look over at the two of them. A family that had just arrived got up and moved to a table a little further away. Robert took a long pull from his glass of beer.

He was the longtime equipment manager for the Braves. He had started working for them part time when he was in high school as a bat boy and worked his way up to his current position. Like Jack, he started out as a fan. Growing up on Commonwealth Avenue, his house was directly between Fenway Park and Braves Field. His whole family were Red Sox fans, but Robert was devoted to the Braves. He stayed with them through the ups, and the mostly downs of last place finishes and washed-up stars on their way out of the league. He was a pretty good baseball player when he was young, but when it was clear a professional career wasn't going to work out for him, he decided the next best thing would be working for his favorite team. He was considered the hardest working equipment manager in the National League. One time in Pittsburgh, he sewed up a hole in first baseman Earl Torgeson's pants in the dugout, while he was still wearing them, just in time for him to go to bat and hit a homerun.

"I'm sorry Bob. I didn't mean anything by it. I can't believe they are actually doing this. I know attendance has been bad, but we just need one more player who will put us over the top. Maybe we can talk them out of this."

"Jack, it's over. The team is gone." He finished his beer.

Jack thought about standing at the top of the dugout after a game and looking out on the empty field. Every time he did, he still felt the same excitement that he had when he went to the stadium for the first time. When he was 10, his father took him on the train into Boston to see the Braves play. Jack always listened to them on the radio, and he had been to some local baseball games before, but nothing compared to this. The size of the stadium with seats as far as the eyes could see, the smell of hot dogs, fried clams, and freshly cut grass, the sound of the bat hitting the ball, and the thousands of people there to watch the game overwhelmed him with excitement. The players seemed larger than life on the field. His favorite, catcher Al López, made everything look so easy on the field. That day he had two hits and threw out a player trying to steal second. After the game, they waited by the locker room exit and watched the players come out. López signed a ball for him on his way by. He knew right then he wanted to be a professional baseball player.

Taking after his hero, Jack played catcher in college for the Holy Cross Crusaders in Worcester. Scouts had been watching him during his junior year, and he talked to them about leaving school a year early to join a Major League team. In a game against Boston College, he came to bat in the eighth inning with men on second and third and the score tied. He knocked a curveball to the left field fence, scoring both runners, but as he was rounding first to make it a double, he felt something in his knee snap. He collapsed on the base path and while he was able to crawl back to first base safely, he couldn't stand up. The team ran over and helped carry him off of the field and into the locker room. He was unable to play for the rest of the season, and he wasn't fully healed until the fall. He came back to the team in the spring, but he wasn't the same. He couldn't squat behind home plate anymore and had to be moved from catcher to first base. He had trouble moving off of the bag to field routine ground balls, and what were once doubles and triples for him were now singles. The Major League teams that were interested in signing him moved on. He was devastated. His dream of being a professional ball player had evaporated, and he didn't know what to do next. He talked to his coach who knew some of the people who worked for the Braves and set him up with a job there. It was the only job he had ever had, and the only job he ever wanted to have. Now, that was in jeopardy. Jack felt betrayed. How could a team he loved so much do this to him? How could they abandon him and the city?

"What about all of the season ticket holders? They already paid for this year."

"They're refunding everyone" said Robert.

"Well, what about the city series? They can't just leave the Red Sox without someone to play against."

"They will figure it out. This is all new still, but I am sure they have a plan. Nothing is going to stop them from taking the team west."

They sat silently for a moment and Robert took another piece of corn bread out of the basket to eat.

Jack looked up at Robert and asked, "What do we do now?"

"Great question" he said motioning to the waitress. He pointed to Jack and said, "Can we get this man a drink?"

"And a clam chowder" Jack added.

The waitress brought over beers for both of them and a chowder.

"I have a friend in New York who works for the Giants," said Jack. "Maybe I will move down there and get a job with them."

"That would be some job security," said Robert. "Can you imagine them ever moving?"

Willie Mays on the Mets, 1972-73

Peter M. Gordon

Mom and Dad thrilled when Mays came to the Mets,
eager to relive New York baseball of their youth.

Forty-one and fading, Mays still showed
flashes of fire that made him world's best

ballplayer for twenty years. Star hurler Tom Seaver
always said Mays was Mets' best player in '72.

Led the team in on base average plus slugging.
By '73, gone his rifle arm that once threw 440 feet

from center field to home on the fly. Gone, too,
speed and power that made him first NL player

to hit thirty homers, steal thirty bases in one season.
Old, he worked hard as always at the game – studied

pitchers, hitters, plays, looking, working for an edge. I saw
Mays on the Mets stumble getting out of the batter's box,

trip, running to field flies, toss baseball to other fielders
to throw back to infield. Will to win, baseball brains,

kept him playing, but when he lost the center field job
to a career .236 hitter, Mays knew his time was over.

Shea Stadium September, Willie Mays Night, Dad and I
heard Willie say goodbye to America. Baseball gods gave

Mays a last act; allowed Mets to eke out a division win.
The world watched Willie hit .300 in the playoffs, with

his last hit, won World Series Game Two, top of inning
twelve - bouncer just out of the third baseman's reach,

line drive in the box score. Fans celebrate Mays' talent
and joy; Mets fans revere his unconquerable will.

Zobrist

Ben Zobrist, Tampa Bay Rays fans' secret star,
our true north, guiding our path to victory.
Like Ringo joining the Beatles, Zobrist made
good teams great, great teams, champions.

Like a great unsigned band found in a hipster
bar frequented Friday nights, we held Zobrist's
greatness close. We knew it was no coincidence
ten years of last place finishes ended in 2008

after Zobrist joined the big club to stay. Twenty-
eight, old for a rookie -- Rays' front office
the first one to see his genius. He played
everywhere in the field, but even in 2011, when

he led all AL players in Wins Above Replacement
Value, he didn't command a top salary or covers of
sports magazines. Rays fans did not care. We loved,
cheered, appreciated, steady, hustling, Ben Zobrist.

We mourned when the Rays traded him in 2015
before he became a free agent. He led the Royals
to a World Series win. Joined his old Rays skipper
Joe Maddon on the Cubs in 2016, earned World

Series MVP as Cubs ended their century-long
Series win drought. Isn't it funny how champion
teams seem to follow Ben around? He finally
belonged to the world cover band that became

the Beatles. Retired now, may never make the Hall
of Fame, but when spring training comes around,
every team's looking for their own Ben Zobrist.
I wear his number 18 jersey to every home game.

Photo Day

George Skornickel

It was a bright, sunny Sunday afternoon, perfect for a baseball game. Unlike other games, this was a special day. It was Pirates photo day. Fans were to be permitted on the field to take photos of all of the players. No autographs were allowed, but we were free to take photos.

I had my trusty Kodak camera as I entered the Forbes Field gate.

At this time in the afternoon the Pirates would have normally been taking batting practice but instead they were seated on folding chairs on top of the dug-out. Behind each player for a backdrop was a large piece of un-painted plywood. At the feet of each player was a placard with each of the player's name. I had looked at my baseball cards, read my yearbook so many times, as well as coming to games regularly, that I didn't need name tags to know who the players were.

The setting was somewhat chaotic. There was no organized line. There were just fans rushing to whatever player they wanted to photograph. I had a different plan. It was my plan to start at the beginning of the line of players and get as many player photos as I could. I had a full roll of film in my camera and another fresh roll in my pocket.

Some of the players seemed bored sitting there. They were all in full uniform except for their hats. I my camera and got ready to start,

The first player in line was Dick Schofield. I snapped a quick picture "Thank you, Mr. Schofield," I said, trying to be friendly. He shifted in his chair like he felt un-comfortable.

Next in line was Donn Clendennon. I realized he was tall but looking up at his sitting on the dug-out with his legs stretched out, his legs seemed even longer than I thought. I took a picture, thanked him, and moved on.

The area in front of the dug-out was getting crowded with people, not all of them polite. I got jostled a few times by people behind me. Why couldn't they just be patient so that all of us could take our pictures.

Just ahead of me there was some sort of commotion from the crowd. People were laughing.

I edged forward to see what was going on. There was a group of people standing in front of Dick Stuart. Stuart wasn't just sitting there. He was busy making all sorts of funny faces for the cameras. I moved closer to the dug-out and got a shot of him and his crazy antics.

I continued down the line to Jim Pagliaroni. He was followed by Dick Groat, Rocky Nelson, Al McBean, and Bill Mazeroski. Finally, I got to the player I had come to photograph. Roberto Clemente. There was a sizable crowd in front of him several persons deep. Most were snapping pictures, others were just standing there, a few asking him questions.

I squirmed to the front of the line and began to shoot pictures. Clemente sat there looking very comfortable, smiling at the fans.

As I stood there after taking my pictures, I noticed something. I was looking at Clemente's hands and wrists. You could see the strength in them. The strength that allowed him to hit line-drive to the outfield for base hits.

I finished taking a few more pictures of the remaining players, took one last look, and started off the field toward my seat.

I later went to many more games, but I don't remember there ever being another photo day like that one with me and my trusty Kodak.

The Miracle of Beans and Whistles

Joseph Stanton

Rube Waddell—famed
for sparring with alligators, Jim Jeffries,
and more than a few umpires;
for trotting off field mid-game,
for playing marbles with kids,
for chasing fire wagons,
for barking at dogs,
for soliciting magic charms from fans—

had his grandest moment in 1903
when he lofted a long foul over the wall
and up onto the roof of the biggest
bean cannery in all of Bean Town,
where the ball, by happenstance,
lodged itself in a steam pipe,

setting the colossal cooker to whistling
so loud that fire captains for miles around
assumed the worst and sounded
their shrill shrieks of alarm.
Just as the clang of fire wagons
and stampedes of fire-fearing fans
added to the din, pressure behind

the pipe-clogged ball built up
and up and up and up. . . until
the massive boiler had to go *kaboom!*—
fountaining scalding brown beans
up and over, raining hot, dark hail
from screaming, sunny-blue skies
down upon bleachers where
fans hysterically wept and wept,

tearing their clothes, wailing
that the end of the world was near,
as Rube Waddell, having circled
the bases, was standing on home plate
shouting at the bewildered umpire
that he would punch him in the nose
if he called his home run a foul ball.

Lift by Kurt Sinclair

Man Verses Nature Versus ESPN at Wrigley Field

Joseph Stanton

On national television
a hawk swooped out of the sky
intent upon a descending pop fly,
thinking it a tasty morsel of white dove,
distracting thereby a rookie center fielder,
unaccustomed as he was
to the attack of predatory raptors.

The scorekeeper ruled it an error
and the TV sportscaster,
oblivious to the attacking bird,
assessed the situation,
saying,
"He just plain missed that one."

Leroy Neiman's Reggie Jackson

Joseph Stanton

Neiman's paintings explode color—
blue, pink, purple, red, green,
and, especially, yellow—
stroked with an extravagance of power,
his brush heavy laden with pigment
primed by the rainbow
and its too vulgar absurdities of glamor.

Neiman strokes,
with evident athleticism,
his overloaded brush,
swinging like Reggie himself,
gripping the instrument
low on the knob,
hitting this one
beautifully,
but way too far over the wall
to be
entirely decorous.

David Freese on Circling the Bases After His Homer Won Game Six

Joseph Stanton

I was
running
on clouds.

Painting by David Holden

Duty Calls

William B. (Bryan) Steverson

A tribute to baseball's Ted "Double Duty" Radcliffe.

Hey Ted!
Are you on the mound today?
Fastballs and curveballs keeping hitters at bay.

Hey Double!
Are you behind the plate today?
"Thou Shalt Not Steal" is what you say.

Hey Mr. Radcliffe!
Are you managing today?
Deciding who sits and those who play.

Hey Duty!
Are you batting cleanup today?
Swatting those baseballs far, far away.

Hey Alex!
How about your brother?
A Negro League star who plays like no other.

Hey Mobile!
Did you remember Duty and Satch?
They were born there in the same briar patch.

Hey Mr. Cobb!
Why the frown on your face?
Has Ted just nailed you stealing second base?

Hey Doc!
Duty's five fingers were broken.
An ugly reminder and a league's lasting token.

Hey Fans!
Who was it you saw?
Duty was there with the best by far.

Hey Jim Crow!
Did you know in Birmingham one day?
Duty showed up with a white man to play.

Hey Cooperstown!
Do you know who awaits your call?
Let him know all about the Hall.

Hey Baseball!
Will you recognize Ted Radcliffe someday?
 Consider his achievements in the times he did play.

Hey St. Peter!
In your world all are the same.
Nothing limits Duty and our wonderful game.

Home at the Stretch

Jared Wyllys

My father got back from the war just before the 7th inning stretch. We sat together about a dozen rows back from the visitors' dugout on the first base side at Wrigley Field on a Friday afternoon a few days after school had let out for the summer, and he had taken me to my first baseball game after I had waited my whole life for him to get home so we could go together.

He had arrived at home in mid-September almost three years ago, when I was still only five. I remember the joy in my mother and then the almost immediate and palpable tension. He was much quieter than I expected, hardly looking at me and rarely speaking to either of us. He didn't drink, raise his voice, or teach me things. On Monday mornings, he would leave in his Chrysler that I was desperate to ride in with him, and then he would return for dinner, eat silently, and then sit by the window facing our street until I went to bed. Five days a week, "good night" were usually the only words he spoke to me. On Saturdays and Sundays, he'd fuss alone in our detached garage. Once after he had been home for about a year, I heard him snort at something he read in the paper, but otherwise he didn't smile, laugh, wrestle with me, or look me in the eye.

For a while at first my mother would suggest that I be patient; he was adjusting to being home. But eventually she said nothing anymore, and I'd see her wiping her eyes over the dishes. We learned to exist together.

My father left for Europe a week and a half before I was born. For my first five years, my mother would show me the two pictures she had of him and tell me about how much he liked to dance with her and about how much he loved the Cubs. He would dance with her anywhere before the war, she said, even sometimes when there wasn't music. And there wasn't a game that he didn't at least scour the box score; otherwise he listened on the radio faithfully all season long.

But then she got pregnant and he had to go to the war.

One of my earliest memories is of my mother turning a baseball game on the radio while waiting for me to fall asleep for an afternoon nap. That was the first time she told me about how much my father would have loved to be sitting there with us, listening.

From then on, she raised me to love baseball too because that way when my father came home, we could bond over it and go to a game. Even though I started begging to go to Wrigley Field when I was four, she would only say that it was for my father to do that. He'll be home soon, she'd say. It took almost a full three years for him to finally do it. Even when the Cubs were playing in the World Series a few weeks after he'd gotten home, my father paid scant attention.

But that Friday afternoon in June when I was eight, he surprised my mother and I both by coming home around lunchtime and telling me to finish eating and come with him to the car. We were going to a baseball game. All he said on the way there was that the Cubs were playing the New York Giants and asked whether or not I knew how to fill out a scorecard.

When we got to our seats and started filling out the lineups, he scowled when I laughed that the Cubs' left fielder's name was Peanuts.

"He served over there," my father said, crossing his arms.

I was afraid to say anything else until the bottom of the third inning when Bill Nicholson tripled home Andy Pafko to break the 1-1 tie. My father smiled -- just with his eyes -- when that happened. I glanced at him and let out a little cheer and clapped my hands together once. He saw out of the corner of his eye and the side of his mouth facing me lifted just a little.

Two innings later, he asked if I liked school. I told him my teacher's and my best friend's names and how we played stickball and tag at recess.

"Hm," he said, with his fingers drumming a little on his knees.

In the bottom of the 6th, the Cubs scored again, making it a 3-1 lead.

"We should leave in a little while," my father said. "There will be traffic."

Wordlessly, he made known that we would wait until the top of the 7th was over to make sure the Giants didn't score before we headed for the car. Ralph Hamner got the first batter to ground out weakly and my father cleared his throat and almost said something. After the next batter grounded out to the shortstop, he spoke again.

"I met a woman overseas," he said, not looking at me. "A French woman."

I wasn't sure what he meant, but I could feel a slight nervousness from him, which was strange. Distant though he had been, my father at least projected confidence in everything he did.

"She spoke only a little English, but it was enough," he went on. "I betrayed your mother over there."

I don't remember the third out of that inning because Wrigley went quiet in my head and the grass and seats and fans into a swirl. I looked over at him. He was finally looking me in the eye.

"I'm not the same with your mother anymore," he said. "I can't be."

After that we walked together to our Chrysler. He put his arm lightly over my shoulder as we went and told me a story about sneaking into his first Cubs game the year they lost the World Series to Philadelphia. He flat out grinned as he told me about eventually getting caught and thrown out.

On the drive home, he lit a cigar and relaxed in his seat when Doris Day and Buddy Clark came on the radio, and we sank into an easy quiet. I was delighted and wished we could drive forever.

As we rounded into our neighborhood, he stopped at an intersection and looked at me, still smiling a little but serious.

"Thanks for coming with me today," he said, adding after a moment: "Son."

The next two blocks I could only think about how we were finally all together again. As we pulled into our driveway, I saw my mother sitting in my father's chair by the front window waiting for us. I saw, too, the quiet grimness return to him, and I realized I wouldn't be the same with her anymore either.

Paintings
Paul Borelli

Here are four of the 32 pieces from my 1947 Series, depicting the best players from the year that Jackie Robinson first played in the majors 75 years ago. These are all 5x7 inches, acrylic on Claybord, done in the style of the Topps poster insert series included in their 1967 baseball card packs. Shown here are Hall of Famers Luke Appling, Warren Spahn, Pee Wee Reese, and Lou Boudreau.

Here are two pieces from my more impressionistic series of portraits, which are all 18x24 inches, acrylic on stretched canvas. On the left is "Vada," depicting Reds outfielder Vada Pinson, and on the right is "OWT," i.e., "Original Wild Thing," depicting Yankees pitcher Ryne Duren.

All of my baseball card paintings are of the "What if?" variety, as in this case a 1907 rookie card for Hall of Famer Walter Johnson and outfielder teammate Clyde Milan done in the style of a 1967 Topps rookie card. This one is 5x7 inches, acrylic on canvas panel.

Here are three more pieces from the impressionistic series: "Popgun Pete" depicting Red Sox infielder Pete Runnels, "Say Hey" depicting Giants Hall of Famer Willie Mays, and "Face" depicting Pirates relief pitcher Roy Face.

Four more "What if?" baseball cards from the Deadball Era, clockwise from top left: Boston Americans outfielder Buck Freeman done in 1962 Topps style, Cubs Hall of Fame second baseman Johnny Evers done in 1963 Topps style, Native American multi-sport superstar Jim Thorpe circa 1915 with the New York Giants done in my own design, and Boston Americans Hall of Fame pitcher Cy Young done in 1961 Topps style. All four of these are 5x7 inches, acrylic on canvas panel.

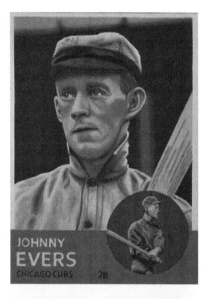

Excerpts on Games 11-19

Jack Buck

Game 11: For today only you've been given the gift of seeing into the future but only for 3 hours max. Don't bother watching. Spend your afternoon napping instead. Happy Sunday you have work tomorrow.

Game 12: The Monday nightmare of a potential week-long losing streak averted. A comeback win. The unpredictability of life emphasized in the bottom of the 9th.

Game 13: Odd devotion to willingly put yourself through. Day Off: No game today so I guess I'll subject myself to writing poems.

Game 14: After a night of appropriate sleep and this morning's strong cup of coffee, I believe in the team again.

Game 15: Well, that sure was painless. I'm going to write a letter to the team to ask them to do more of that.

Game 16: If you drink enough beers from the outfield bleachers maybe that big fat zero up there on the scoreboard will manifest itself into an 8.

Game 17: Contingent on cooperation like not swinging on 3-0 and happily taking a walk.

Game 18: Trudging along from one seared plateau to the next as expectations fade away in a mirage.

Game 19: Turn down for what!

Take Me Out to the Ball Game on 2020, A Season's Eulogy

Duane Victor Keilstrup

Not every fan has seen baseball Hall-of-Famers (or even potential ones), play in person; and not every fan today, especially younger ones, have sung or perhaps even heard the baseball anthem "Take Me Out to the Ball Game," with lyrics by Jack Norworth and music by Albert von Tilzer.

To remedy such problems, young as well as older fans can go to several helpful online histories of the song. But perhaps the best history is found in MLB's official historian and SABR stalwart

John Thorn's 2013 "Our Game" MLB Blog reference to George Boziwick's "Take Me Out to the Ball Game: The Story of Katie Casey and Our National Pastime."[1] Everything from the genesis and steady development of the song to become the baseball anthem to its implication of progress in women's involvement in baseball can be found in Boziwick's piece which appeared in Base Ball: A Journal of the Early Game (Vol. 6, No. 2, Fall 2012). The song's chorus, originally resonant for Katie Casey [probably influenced by Norworth's girlfriend Trixie Friganza, and no connection to Casey in Ernest Thayer's "Casey at the Bat"], now resonates with the sustained message that baseball is for everyone, regardless of class, gender, or generation. This inclusiveness has allowed "Take Me Out to the Ball Game" to achieve a lasting and cherished position of popularity, alongside "Happy Birthday" and the "Star Spangled Banner."

The song's chorus has been performed countless times on radio, TV, recordings, in movies, and has appeared in children's books, commercials, and promotions. While there are at least 30 sheet music versions, we know that Norworth wrote a slightly updated version in 1927, the year the Babe hit his 60 home runs. Later in 1934 the song was officially performed at a MLB game and gradually became more and more popular, becoming something of a seventh inning tradition by 1946. Then in 1977[2] Chicago White Sox fans began to sing the song along with Harry Caray after owner Bill Veeck had convinced

---

1 George Boziwick "Take Me Out to the Ball Game: The Story of Katie Casey and Our National Pastime," *Our Game*, Blog, October 8, 2013. https://ourgame.mlblogs.com/take-me-out-to-the-ball-game-the-story-of-katie-casey-and-our-national-pastime-c8f76a0fc6ba

2 Anna Laymon "The Feminist History of 'Take Me Out to the Ballgame," *Women Who Shaped History*, Blog. *Smithsonian Magazine*. October 10, 2019, updated July 14, 2020. https://www.smithsonianmag.com/history/feminist-history-take-me-out-ball-game-180973307/

him to turn his broadcast microphone on. That probably sealed its singing at baseball games across America as the official baseball anthem.

Here are the complete original song lyrics from 1908 and 1927 [a "sou" was French slang for penny]:

1908 *Version*

Katie Casey was baseball mad.
Had the fever and had it bad;
Just to root for the hometown crew,
Ev'ry sou Katie blew.
On a Saturday, her young beau
Called to see if she'd like to go
To see a show, but Miss Kate said,
"No, I'll tell you what you can do."

"Take me out to the ball game,
Take me out with the crowd.
Buy me some peanuts and cracker jack,
I don't care if I never get back,
Let me root, root, root for the home team,
If they don't win it's a shame.
For it's one, two, three strikes, you're out,
At the old ball game."

Katie Casey saw all the games,
Knew the players by their first names;
Told the umpire he was wrong,
All along good and strong.
When the score was just two to two,
Katie Casey knew what to do,
Just to cheer up the boys she knew,
She made the gang sing this song

1927 *Version*

Nelly Kelly loved baseball games,
Knew the players, knew all their names,
You could see her there ev'ry day,

Shout "Hurray," when they'd play.
Her boyfriend by the name of Joe
Said, "To Coney Isle, dear, let's go,"
Then Nelly started to fret and pout,
And to him I heard her shout:

"Take me out to the ball game,
Take me out with the crowd.
Buy me some peanuts and cracker jack,
I don't care if I never get back,
Let me root, root, root for the home team,
If they don't win it's a shame.
For it's one, two, three strikes, you're out,
At the old ball game."

Nelly Kelly was sure some fan,
She would root just like any man,
Told the umpire he was wrong,
All along, good and strong.
When the score was just two to two,
Nelly Kelly knew what to do,
Just to cheer up the boys she knew,
She made the gang sing this song:

"Take me out to the ball game,
Take me out with the crowd.
Buy me some peanuts and cracker jack,
I don't care if I never get back,
Let me root, root, root for the home team,
If they don't win it's a shame.
For it's one, two, three strikes, you're out,
At the old ball game."

This is introduction to the following 2020 COVID 19 tongue-in-cheek
version of the song's chorus. This version may no doubt soon be purposefully
forgotten by most, along with other fallout from that year of the worldwide
pandemic, but to some faithful baseball fans in 2020, like me, without tragic

personal losses it may remain an appropriate season's eulogy, especially for losing teams like the Texas Rangers who had the most losses of any American League team in 2020.

TAKE ME OUT TO THE BALL GAME, A 2020 EULOGY

Take me out to the ball game.
Out with all the fake crowd,
Buy me some peanuts and a Ranger face mask.
I did not care if I ever got back,
but I'd root, root, root for the Rangers
Though losing sure was a shame,
It was 1, 2, 3 strikes and out
at the COVID ball game!

Turning Back the Clock: Rediscovering Baseball Cards

Ryan Isaac

I needed to put the cards down already. Needed to, but I couldn't. I recognized the feeling — it had been 30 years since it visited me: the undeniable power of baseball cards to overwhelm the need for sleep.

Things were different now, though. Very different. Before too long, a toddler would be waking up, completely indifferent to the fact that his father's joy for an old hobby had been unexpectedly rekindled after lying dormant for decades.

It was the best non-medical news of the pandemic: I learned that the baseball card market is once again popular and thriving. In fact, many cards are more valuable than ever.

About three years ago, I packed up my baseball cards from my childhood bedroom, just prior to a cross-country move to San Diego. At the time, I can remember thinking about the Mickey Mantle rookie card. You know, the 1952 Topps 2-1/16" x 3-1/8" piece of cardboard that defined a generation. Seemingly everyone who was a kid in the '50s possessed the card only to have their mother throw it out or give it to the kid down the street who put it in his bike spokes.

When I was packing up my cards — stored thoughtfully but not hermetically in 800-count storage boxes, old wax-pack cases, and random boxes into which my cards fit in a Tetris-like manner — I kept thinking about the newspaper articles that both my grandfathers shared with me during my active card-buying days. Every year, there was another story detailing how baseball cards outpaced the S&P 500. Data supported the hobby as a sound investment. Then, in the late '80s, card production increased significantly and saturated the market.

For the last three or four years, though, baseball cards — and trading cards in general — have rallied. All it took was the pandemic lifestyle to give the industry an additional push.

Neglected as they may have been, I was nonetheless tethered to them after years of devotion. They were always there for me. The fronts of the cards put faces to names, while the backs offered the statistics and insights that fed my cravings and curiosities. I alphabetized them, ordered them by number, by team, by year; I displayed them around my room. But as I grew older and the market — flooded with more and more brands, editions, and gimmicks — flatlined, I didn't know if I even wanted them anymore. I just didn't know what I'd ever do with them.

It was the monetization of baseball cards that ended the innocence of my youth.

Sometime in 1985, I walked into Jay's Sports Connection. Of course, my friends and I weren't there for baseball cards. It was the peak of Garbage Pail Kids mania, and the word on the playground was that Jay's had the trash.

I remember standing shoulder-to-shoulder with other kids in a bit of a scrum, each of us jockeying for the attention of the store employees: Jay, whose name was on the sign outside, and a man named Uncle Dave, whose t-shirt advertised that moniker. Classmates of mine who were indoctrinated collectors seemed to speak a different language within the store's confines. When I had my chance to speak to Uncle Dave — a man who might have a case against The Simpsons if he sued the show for creating Comic Boy Guy in his likeness — he told me that the rubber bands I had around my cards would decrease their value by potentially warping, bending, or tearing them.

Farewell, childhood. It was a good nine-year run.

Immediately, the joy of collecting baseball cards became competitive, objectively measurable, and financially motivated. Hey, it also turned out that the baseball sticker collections I had were worthless because I actually stuck them in the book. Go figure.

Until recently, my cards had been resting peacefully in a built-in cabinet, clinging to their real estate before beach towels or spare sheets uprooted them.

Well, it's a brand-new day now, and the towels, sheets, family photo albums, and my wife's yearbooks better watch how they speak to those precious baseball cards.

Before we go any further, I want to make something clear. I imagine that reading about someone meticulously going through his baseball cards is only slightly more enjoyable than enduring someone else's story about a day of frustrating air travel. Similarly, nobody ever says, "So tell me about your fantasy baseball team." I'll keep it simple.

The cards I've accumulated over the years have been reborn. Even better, friendships have a new spark. I text and talk with college friends – a group that had purchased its last packs of cards well before we ever set foot on campus – about the cards we've rediscovered, the inadvertent and unavoidable wear-and-tear that has occurred, and the individual and collective joy we've received from this emotional windfall. The best part is that none of us expected any financial gain from our collections. If a little comes our way, terrific, but realize that this wasn't even a consideration in 2020.

While age has rounded some once-sharp corners and knocked all of us down a grade or two from mint condition, time has rewarded us with the ability to receive a kind of joy that I had previously believed was shattered that day at Jay's.

My grandfather had a common refrain that he would use to punctuate many of the stories he told me: "I thought you'd get a kick out of that." His voice and that line have been echoing in my head all week, a gift in and of itself. The meaning for me in this context is to acknowledge that a card I had forgotten about long ago and that I never considered to have market value now carries a three- or four-digit price tag… in mint condition.

But here's the deal with card condition.

When my son was a little over one year old, he was crawling around on his big sister's bed. Like every good negligent-father story goes, I took my eye off him for one second, then saw him in midair, fear in his eyes (and mine) as he rotated towards the ground. Guess what? My son is still in mint condition. Better than ever, in fact. But if you treat a baseball card that way, goodbye value.

I expect every card I find to be flawed one way or another. Some cards, though, survived only to have been doomed from the start by being cut poorly. This wasn't a rare occurrence either, especially in cards from the '70s and '80s. Who was cutting for Topps back then, Angel Hernandez?

A 1980 Topps Rickey Henderson rookie card in "Gem-Mint 10" condition sold for $180,000 in February 2021. I'm sorry. Did I bury the lede? This sale was what initially got my attention, too. (Prior to the pandemic, the card was selling somewhere between $20,000-$35,000.)

"Mint 9" versions of the same Henderson card have been selling for about $5,000. So you see what just one slight imperfection in centering or coloring can do.

Staying up too late flipping through baseball cards has been the carefree distraction I didn't even know I needed as we commemorate one year of social distancing. I've recaptured the wonderment and joy of a 40-year-old pursuit. I never spent a lot of money on cards as a kid. I remember not buying the 1985 Don Mattingly Topps card for $11 because it just felt like too much to spend. (In mint condition, it's selling for about $400 now — oops.)

I plunked down $7 at a card show on a Jim Abbott rookie card sometime in 8th grade. It was a big decision for me, especially since Beckett Baseball Card Monthly — the pricing bible of the day — listed it at $6. It recently sold for more than $100.

As I flip through my older cards, I'm amazed both at the generally good condition most of them are in and also how so many of them look like 10s at first glance only to reveal a slightly frayed corner or two.

I managed to uncover a handful of cards from 1980 that look to be in mint condition. How those cards survived my entire childhood in that shape is beyond me. (Having only a younger sister who had no interest in them definitely helped.) There are also plenty with unsightly creases and folds to be found. I still remember sitting on my Mattingly rookie. That was a mistake.

Still, I stay up too late on account of baseball cards. I've been energized remembering the feel of the wax pack, sensing the thrill of quickly scanning through the cards for the first time, smelling the gum and seeing its powdery residue. I'll probably do it again tomorrow, too.

I thought you'd get a kick out of that.

Painting by David Holden

Precious Portraits

Bruce Harris

From 1962-1976, Tommy Harper played for eight different teams in the major leagues. His lifetime batting average is .257. He hit 146 home runs, drove in 567 runs, and stole 408 bases, including league-leading totals of 73 (in 1969) and 54 (in 1973) while playing for the Seattle Pilots and Boston Red Sox, respectively. In 1965, he appeared on Topps baseball card number 47.

Fred Gladding was a pitcher for the Detroit Tigers and Houston Astros. During a 13-year career, he won 48 games, lost 34, with an ERA of 3.13. His 29 saves led the National League in 1969. In 1965, he appeared on Topps baseball card number 37.

Flipping baseball cards 56 years ago was serious business. There were many choices from which to choose. One method, albeit never a neighborhood favorite, was standing face-to-face with your opponent, holding (horizontally) the card by its edges with thumb and middle-finger tips. With arm held straight down, dangling at the hip, the card is released. It flips over and over before settling on the ground. A "heads" or "tails" match wins. Flippers also scaled cards against a wall. Closest to the wall (with or without leaners) wins.

Flipping in its most popular form consisted of holding a fistful of cards face-down. One-by-one the cards are turned over and placed between the two flippers. Rules varied. The contestants could be matching players' positions, their teams, players' first (or last) initials, or colors. Colors was my game of choice. In 1965, color matching might be the card's bottom border color (the Yankees cards were purple, Senators green, Cubs red, Phillies blue, etc.). 1965 also featured a small pennant on the card fronts showcasing team names. Colors of these pennants varied depending on team (yellow, white, orange, blue).

Rules were agreed upon beforehand. For example, "no sames" meant a flipper who matched an opponent's card with the same player could not take the pot. A duplicate card is not a valid match. The card pile between the two contestants grew and the flipping continued. Another rule, "no take-outs," haunts me to this day. It was one of the worst agreements I've made in my life. "No take-outs" means just that. A flipper could not remove a card from the game for any reason.

That brings me to Tommy Harper, the one card missing from my collection. I had all the stars, Mays, Mantle, Koufax, Aaron, Banks, Clemente, etc. Yet I remained a single card away from a complete set. No matter how many packs I purchased, no Harper. I couldn't work out a trade for him. The demand always included my lone Mantle card, and that was not going to happen. I yearned to fill-in the open checkbox on that first series checklist card. It haunted me. Small as the open box was, it appeared as a gaping hole in my mind. On the other hand, there was Fred Gladding. I don't know if Topps produced more Fred Gladding cards than Tommy Harper cards, but I had no trouble obtaining Gladding. Fact is, I couldn't avoid him. It seemed as though every other pack I purchased contained Fred Gladding. I have nothing against Fred Gladding. But, his smiling portrait called out, "Yup, me again." Tommy Harper's smile was warm, welcoming, but out of reach.

And suddenly, there he was! Tommy Harper! Staring up at me from the top of the pot. I tried maintaining an air of nonchalance, a poker face, but my racing heart had other ideas. I had to win this pot. And guess what? I did! My collection was complete. Or was it? I had agreed to "no take-outs." I couldn't remove the Harper card from the game. It was mine, but my opponent and I were also playing under strict "no take-aways" rules, which means you played until one player was wiped out. No quitting while winning.

My luck turned south after the Harper pot. I was forced to play him. Eventually, I ran out of cards during an active pot. The (unwritten) rules stated the player who is wiped out picks up the pot of cards, face-up. The flipper plays the card from the bottom of the pot, while the opponent continues feeding the pot with new cards. In my case, if I lost this hand it was game over. I had no cards left to play. Everything, including the Tommy Harper currently in my hand was at stake. I brought cards up from the bottom, hoping for a color match. Again and again. And then, a match! Red on red. I won! Not so fast. I pulled Fred Gladding from the bottom and matched him to another Fred Gladding! "No sames," remember. The game continued, but at that point, the outcome was preordained. The specific details are fuzzy, other than I lost and walked away empty-handed.

I never did obtain a Tommy Harper card that year. I see they sell for about a dollar online these days. That equates to twenty 5-cent packs of cards in 1965, none of which I'm sure contain number 47.

"What Happened Was…" or, Why I Still Love the Game Even Though I Sucked

Adam Young

I didn't know much about baseball when my Mom took me to the Broken Arrow Recreation Department to sign me up for little league in the spring of 1985. I was six years old. I'd never even played catch with a real baseball. I might've swung a broomstick a time or two in my grandparents' yard. All I knew was my brother had played little league the previous year, so I wanted to, too. Luckily, I had brought my plastic glove because when Mom had finished filling the forms, we were immediately taken outside into the noonday sunshine where I was given a quick tryout by one of the Rec Department staffers who told me he'd throw me a little pop-fly just to see what kind of skills I had. He wanted to see how I caught the ball and threw it back. He asked me if I was ready, but it was so bright, I had trouble looking up at him. I was struggling just to keep my eyes open. But I must've nodded my head because he stepped back and said, "Okay, remember, use both hands, but don't let your bare fingers get in the way." Mom looked nervous but tried to reassure me, probably because I was about as not ready as it was possible to be, but I could sense the correct answer to the question was Yes. I must've nodded. "Okay," the guy said. "Here we go." Then he underhanded the ball maybe eight feet into the air, arcing skyward toward me. I'm convinced that day in 1985 had to have been the brightest day in recorded history. And I know I was positioned facing the sun. Plus, I believe I suffered from a rare undiagnosed condition that made it impossible for me, between the ages of 4 and 10, to keep my eyes open on sunny days between the hours of 9 and 2. Some of my most painful childhood memories are of having my picture taken and being unable to open my eyes. Anyway, if no medical professionals have yet discovered this bizarre condition, I'm more than happy to contribute my anecdotal experience to help identify it. It was especially bad on Easter Sundays and Christmas mornings when my Mom forced my older brother and me to wear itchy and uncomfortable matching polyester suits and wool sweaters then stand away from the shadows of the porch looking directly into piercing sunlight for interminable minutes while she found the perfect angle with her Polaroid. Anyway, that spring day when I took my first tryout and I looked up at exactly high noon and those ominous church bells began tolling and the brightest sun ever recorded was bearing straight down on me, and my vision was flooded with white light, I did what any six year-old who'd never caught a real baseball would do: I took cover under my glove, made my face small, closed my eyes even tighter, and braced for impact. Jose Canseco, I feel you. Of course, it hurt. I took it right on the forehead. But I was mostly crying because I was sure I'd messed up and wasted everybody's time. There was no way they'd let me play now. Who did I think was, trying out for baseball when I'd never even held a real bat or thrown a real ball?

But then I heard the staffer tell Mom, "Okay, we've got a team for him. Let's get him sized for a uniform." I couldn't believe it. It was amazing. It was impossible to mess up any more than I had, to be any more untrained and incompetent than I had been, but they still had a uniform waiting for me? And it was a great uniform, too: a black V-neck with a yellow-and-white collar and matching piping on the sleeves. Our team name, Bandits, was screen-printed in cursive across the front. They even gave me a real baseball cap, a yellow adjustable with a mesh back and cloth front with a capital B (like the B in the Braves font) stitched in black. Just like that, I was on the team. I'd done it! That uniform was easily the single best outfit I'd ever owned, which wasn't saying much, I guess, but for the first 10-12 years of my life, until I outgrew my older brother, only the socks and underwear were really mine. Nearly everything I else I wore were hand-me downs from my brother and older cousins. But my baseball uniform was like none of the itchy suits and sweaters Mom had fought me to wear to church every Sunday. The pants were like stretchy black sweatpants with this cool gold-and-white-striped waistband that matched the gold and-white-stripes down the seams. And they gave us actual stirrup socks, which seemed incomprehensible and pointless. Who would've guessed that such a thing as stirrup socks actually existed? Their sole purpose seemed to be symbolic, like barristers' wigs. Which was the genius of them. Even now, I want to start wearing stirrup socks and short pants. Why not? Just to remind the world, "I know I'm a dorky old dude, but I, too, was once a ballplayer." Then we actually played a few games, and thankfully, I don't remember much, except for one at bat. I remember digging into the dirt of the batter's box, wearing the same white tennis shoes I wore to school, the ones with the wide flat fluorescent orange-and-black argyle shoe-laces, which was the fad then. Coach Franke couldn't have stood more than 12 or 15 feet away, if that. He lobbed me a few underhanded tosses, apologizing for the bad ones and encouraging me to swing at the good ones. We were allowed as many pitches as we wanted, but after five missed swings you were out. At some point I actually hit a ground ball and ran. It was among the greatest moments of my childhood, which was never bad or traumatic, but which rarely got much better than that. So, I started to like it, not just the uniform or being on a team, but baseball itself, the game, and the distinctive fears and fun that it engendered. For one thing, in the field, the ball never came to me (and I definitely never went to it), so defense was easy. You just stood in the grass and watched either the other team striking out or your teammates converging on the ball while you listened to parents yelling and clapping and while you smelled cigarette smoke on the breeze and waited for your turn to hit. Then you ran to the dugout and drank water and chewed Big League Chew and sat on the bench with kids your age going through the same thing, kids who, even if they weren't your best friends, exactly, were at least fellow sufferers wearing the same uniform. Then, when it was all over, which didn't take too long, the parents gave you a Pepsi and a Snickers bar. I didn't think it could get any better. But then, near the end of that first little league season, Coach Franke told us he'd been trying to arrange a team dinner and had invited Bill Russell. We were more excited about that than we'd been about the 2 or 3 times we'd actually hit the ball all season. We high-fived each other, shouted "Hooray," and then we were all quiet for a few seconds until somebody finally asked Coach Franke the question the rest of us hadn't even realized we should be asking yet: "Who's Bill Russell?"

This was early 1985, and while Broken Arrow might have been one of the fastest growing suburbs of Tulsa, I bet we couldn't have counted on two hands the number of professional athletes we knew by name. I knew Joe Montana and Dan Marino from a Super Bowl book I'd bought at the book fair. And everybody had heard of Babe Ruth. I remembered one kid at school who claimed Mickey Mantle was his great-uncle, which was probably true since Mantle had been born in Spavinaw and raised in Commerce, towns just a few counties away. But back then, I didn't know who Mickey Mantle was. The point is, I doubt any of us had ever watched a full major league baseball game before, either on television or in person. Maybe a couple of us had actually been to a minor-league game (the Rangers' Double-A affiliate, the Drillers, played nearby in Tulsa), but I don't think any of us had even heard of Bill Russell, much less knew who he was or what it meant to get to meet him. And now that I think about it, that moment was probably the first time I'd ever heard of the Dodgers. It was an awakening. Aside from "getting saved" the year before when I learned that I could die at any moment, in the blink of an eye, and that I was a born sinner doomed for everlasting torment in a bottomless pit of flames, separated for all eternity from God and family and anybody or anything even remotely loving or pleasant if I didn't confess my sins and ask Jesus into my heart that very night—you know, aside from that—learning about Bill Russell and the Dodgers was the 2nd great consciousness-expanding moment of my childhood. Coach Franke explained that Bill Russell had been the Dodgers' starting shortstop since before we were born and that for the past fifteen years, he'd spent his off-seasons living in our town, in Broken Arrow, Oklahoma. Unfortunately, a few weeks later, after our last game that summer, Coach Franke huddled us up around a cooler behind the dugout to break the bad news: Bill Russell wasn't going to be able to meet with us after all. Instead, to celebrate our year, we'd all be going to a Drillers game, but if we were lucky, Mr. Russell might have a souvenir to give each of us who were able to make it. The night of the game, Coach Franke met us near the ticket booth to hand out the souvenirs. It was incredible, a special delivery from a major league ballplayer. I had no idea what to expect when he reached into a brown paper sack and pulled out a plastic-wrapped Dodgers sweatband, which I immediately ripped out of the package and proudly wore all summer, even to Sunday School, just in case, because you never knew when Tommy Lasorda might call you up. You had to be ready. To this day, it's among the coolest things I've ever owned, and it hurts that I no longer have it, stretched and sweat-stained and stuffed in a drawer somewhere. I was so small back then, the wristband covered half my forearm. It had two blue stripes on either end with a wider white stripe in the middle, and inside the white stripe was that Dodgers logo, the cursive script with the ball flying through it. I knew what that ball meant. I still had the knot on my head to prove it. I knew you had to be tough to play this game. Either that, or you had to know when to get out of the way, which is why they were called the Dodgers, I assumed. Anyway, the wristbands were probably left over from a ticket promotional during the season, but that didn't matter, and was actually cooler. To think they'd come all that way from Dodger Stadium to suburban Oklahoma by way of Bill Russell himself, no less! Wow! Who cared that they didn't match our black and gold Bandits uniforms? That wristband had been bestowed upon me, like a gift from the gods, and I treasured it by never taking it off, even in the shower. That's how you cleaned it. My mom has a picture of me wearing it with a pink and gray Hawaiian shirt at some botanical garden in Muskogee. In the picture, I'm standing there with my arm around the neck of a miniature dinosaur statue (which is ironically huge, since it's a dinosaur), and there I am, casually showing off my wristband, as if to say to myself all these years later, "I may not be able to see you, Future Self, since I can't even keep my eyes open long enough to take this picture, but, Ladies and Gentlemen, I was once, and forever will be, a ballplayer. If you don't believe me, ask Bill Russell." All I needed was some eye black, and I would've had it made.

Painting by David Holden

Hinchliffe Stadium

Donna Muscarella

The Year 2020 was filled with both triumph and tragedy. The same could be said about the Negro Leagues, born out of the tragedies of racism and "Jim Crow" laws and triumphing as a professional baseball organization fueled by entrepreneurship and the talents of men and women who were excluded from Major League Baseball merely because of the color of their skin.

During the Negro Leagues centennial celebration, which coincidentally encompassed most of 2020, I discovered Hinchliffe Stadium: one of the few Negro Leagues ballparks still standing. Despite the stadium being located approximately ten miles from my home and having parked my car right next to Hinchliffe numerous times while photographing the Paterson Great Falls, I was oblivious to the fact that the structure had served as a ballpark, let alone one of such historic significance.

Hinchliffe Stadium has its own stories of triumph and tragedy. It was built and opened in the throes of the Great Depression. It served the Negro Leagues well as the home ballpark for the New York Black Yankees and New York Cubans and host of the 1933 Colored World Series. Larry Doby was discovered there by the Newark Eagles while playing high school ball for Paterson Eastside. After the Negro Leagues left Hinchliffe, the stadium stood for many years as an attractive venue for sports and cultural events. Sadly, use of the stadium declined over time. The once-celebrated venue sat dormant for years in a state of disrepair and neglect. The images shared here were captured at the end of that era. They offer the opportunity to reminisce about what was and dream of what may be as a massive restoration of Hinchliffe is underway.

The Mediocre Middle-Aged Shortstop

Paul Moorehead

pitch passes apex, figured like physics
crouch creaks through knees and neck
and dirt gentle taps at careworn glove
reminds it waits just underneath
a quick bat wakes the play, except your drowsy feet
and the ball spins by, sprints by too lively
gone to wind down in the outfield grass

thinking that last play like it's still ticking
timing every next thing like it's got a fuse
quiet looper over second, reading it sideways
backpedaling at a tilt on stammering spikes
reaching overhead, the ball unseen but felt glancing
then bounce and stagger in the dirt like it's unwound

that askew chance faded like last summer's falls
of feet less fleet than twilight shaded
a step — maybe two — up the tricksy middle
middle and crack! a top-spun grounder
through the pitcher, sprawled, but smack! into my mitt
to hand to flippant arc to ready second
— maybe seconds — in plenty of time and damn all the clocks!

SABR Members Ride the Card Art Wave

Jason A. Schwartz

One of the more noteworthy trends during the COVID-19 pandemic was the rise of "card art," defined here as art created from or in the style of baseball cards. Leading the effort have been official releases from Topps, namely Project 2020 and Project 70. However, a number of independent artists, including several SABR members, have sharpened their scissors and X-Acto knives or their digital equivalents to add their own pieces into this growing slice of the Hobby.

My personal medium of choice has been glitter paper, available in large sheets from art supply shops. As an amateur baseball card historian and co-chair of SABR's Baseball Cards Research Committee, I enjoy paying homage to the Hobby's classic sets such as 1933 Goudey, but the cards I work on most often are the cards I grew up with in the 1980s. Many of these cards are referred to pejoratively as Junk Wax due to excessive overproduction, but that doesn't diminish the sentimental value they hold among many collectors my age.

The popularity of the cards I've made, under the name Heavy J Studios, has allowed me to raise more than $15,000 for charity during the pandemic.

Two of my fellow SABR Chicago chapter members, Chris Kamka and John Racanelli, have entered the Card Art arena as well. John has enjoyed great popularity online with his Literal Series, but also reimagines popular players in the 1949 Leaf style or even as old school video game cartridges. While John occasionally breaks out the scissors and glue, most of his pieces are created digitally. using Photoshop.

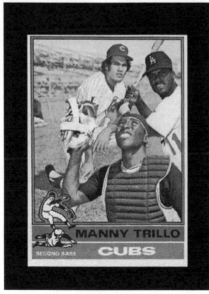

Chris employs a mix of techniques in his Card Art, such as replacing the standard border of this 1988 Topps Nolan Ryan with a dozen or so Fleer Astro stickers or taking the 1987 Topps faux wood border design to its logical extreme.

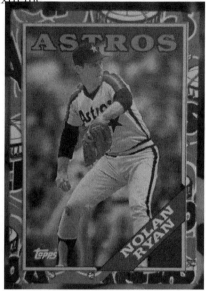 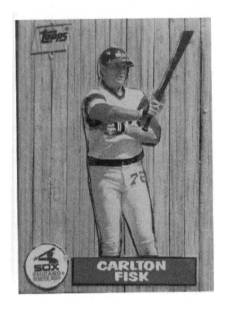

For Bob Davids chapter member Adam Korengold, who I met through our common interest in Card Art, the tools of the trade are a paintbrush and acrylics, as showcased in his pieces "Beautiful Places" and "Childish Bambino at Carnival." Adam also brought Card Art to the SABR mainstream by presenting on the subject at a virtual chapter meeting.

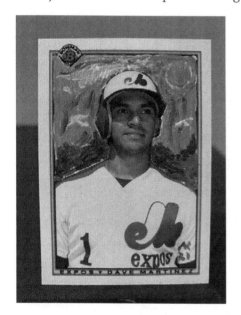

A brand new SABR member who is one of the biggest names in Card Art is Mike Bryan, known in social media spheres as Obi Wan Jabroni.

Mike, who is with the Buck O'Neil (Tallahassee) chapter, gained renown for Project 1991, a spoof of the Topps Project 2020 that used Fleer's yellow-bordered debacle of a set from 1991, and his humorous takes on players from baseball's PED scandals, such as his Rafael Palmeiro Congressional Hearing card. Humor aside, Mike also uses his art to raise money for important causes, most recently leading a team of fellow Card Artists that raised more than $7000 for the Alzheimer's Association.

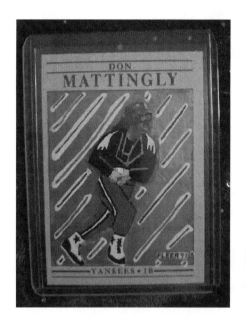

Another heavy hitter in the Alzheimer's fundraising effort was Todd Clark, a new member in our Ted Williams (San Diego) chapter. He is best known for his "Rad Dude" series and posts under the social media handle Lunchmade.

Brian Mazmanian, from our Boston chapter, is another new SABR member who puts new twists on old card designs, in this case the Topps football and baseball flagship sets from 1977. You can find Brian's work on Twitter under the handle @weirdsportmerch.

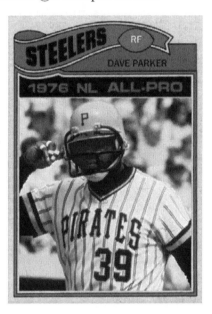

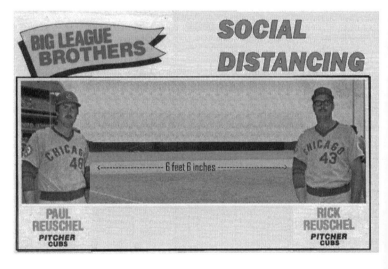

Benjamin Sabin is a member of the Lefty O'Doul (San Francisco Bay Area) chapter of SABR and draws inspiration for his "Cheap Seats" creations from the popular baseball card sets of the early 20th century. In these two examples, Benjamin has reimagined the 1869 Red Stockings team as tobacco cards circa 1910 and Doris Sams of the AAGPBL as a 1914-15 Cracker Jack-style card.

Finally, Paul Ember of our Connie Mack (Philadelphia) chapter, is a SABR member whose drawings highlighted my social media feed even before I thought of Card Art as "a thing." Many of his creations tell a story, such as his 1974 Topps-inspired card of Hank Aaron's mother and his "Cup of Coffee" series depicting "cup of coffee" big leaguers like John Paciorek on actual cups of coffee!

While many Hobby purists turn their noses at Card Art, there is no denying that it spread almost as fast as the coronavirus during the pandemic. From my own experience, I will offer that its infectiousness draws as much from the process as the end result. There is something remarkably therapeutic about the careful cutting required, just as there is a genuine kinship and connection many of us Card Artists feel as we create and share our work.

It's hard to say how much the Card Art movement, inside or outside of SABR, will continue to grow once the pandemic ends and genuine opportunities to gather face-to-face return. What I can say is that in the year of COVID, Card Art proved to be just what the doctor ordered: a chance to interact with our collections in a new way, rediscover our creativity, and make new friends without ever leaving the house.

Becoming The Bambino

Kyle Newman

Babe Ruth is the only man in baseball history
to end the World Series
on a boneheaded caught stealing.

The next season, Ruth hit 60 homers —
Let's see any son of a bitch top that! he shouted
in the clubhouse afterward —
and the '27 Yanks became legendary.

So who cares if, in '26, little Johnny Sylvester
was actually sick or not.
Ruth's three homers in Game 4
were the called shots before
the called shot, and Johnny got walking

to later make his loot in packing machinery.
He died at an old 74, in 1990, eight months
before I was born: When I came into this world
with a cigar, ready to defy sabermetrics
and hoping a horse's kick to the head
would also lead me to The Bambino.

The Grip

Kyle Newman

The day after the season ended I was finally ready to admit my depression,
like the sadness of 27 summers of not winning the division compounded
into the longest late-September Monday in history.
The morning traffic wanted
to gridlock me into reflection. I knew there'd never be the same team
twice,
or two exact at-bats, failure as unique as fingerprints and the nostalgic
forces
I've always relied on: cutting the grass as the radio emanates the pinball
ongoing at Coors, the injecting of myself into the broadcast
just to imagine the ability to keep the same face after a K as a homer.
Years later,
I still see myself with trouble sleeping, all the baseballs in my garage likely
to sprout legs to steal crooked bases in my dreams. And after another
season
we believed was going to turn out differently, I'll cover the diamond
with a see-through plastic, in total darkness, and turn on all the sprinklers.

Pitching Lessons

Kyle Newman

Beside a white rubber
on a small mound of arcana,
I explain the great labor
is to focus without
thinking too much.

My son and I are pitching
straight into the sunrise.
The mesas stand guard
and we pause between heaters
at the rhythm of the geese
circling local parks
to call balls and strikes.

Who knows how much he hears
with all the light in his ears:
I remind him it takes decades
to master this craft. That
the idea is for the pitch
to come out of the hand
and reappear at the plate
as something entirely different:

The mirror of a young father
trying hard, a cutting yarn cake
pretending to be a meatball.

Card Paintings

Adam Korengold

Adam began making card paintings in acrylic on vintage baseball cards, dating from the 1960s to the 2020s, to bring new life to pieces which are more typically considered to be ephemera. He draws inspiration from Russian iconography, color field paintings, and other movements in art and design to create unique, playful, and elegant miniature paintings. It has been a much-loved way to pass the time during the continuing pandemic.

America's Lastime: The Final Days of Baseball

Justin Klugh

All right; welcome, welcome.

If you're standing here, then you received a summons from the Department of Movement and Leisure to perform your required monthly act of recreation and/or exercise.

You may be wondering why this month you were mandated to show up at a ramshackle series of hallways in upstate New York that have been partially reclaimed by nature. Well, it's my job to inform you that you are on the final tour *ever* of the National Baseball Hall of Fame here in Cooperstown.

Please stop groaning. Anyone who groans too loudly will have to leave, your enjoyment will not be logged in in the database, and you will have to find a source of movement or leisure elsewhere. Also, it hurts my feelings.

Thank you. Let's begin. If you'll follow me this way...

You may notice a shocking lack of baseball-related materials here at The Hall. Baseball's origins are basically just a multi-century game of whisper down the lane played exclusively with folklore, hate, and lies. As wave after wave of public health crises hit our society and shut down the concept of "outside," our executives and curators felt that, given our financial state, much of the museum could be sold off. So, it was determined that the National Baseball Hall of Fame could give you the full experience of the sport by glossing over its history and focusing almost exclusively on its destruction.

For those of you who weren't groaning, "baseball" was a sport played with balls, sticks, drugs, and a fluctuating set of increasingly incoherent rules. Historians have long debated the specific origins of the game that would come to be called the nation's "pastime," but after generations of endless research and documentation, we can say with high confidence that it was invented by small, pasty children who were too sickly or physically weak to play any of the other, cooler childhood games of the 1800s, like "Punch the Weakling," "Farm chores," "Survive polio," or "Kill the Weakling."

Playing baseball, these malnourished youths would attract quite the crowd in time, with their flailing and running and shouting. In fact, it rocketed in popularity with such swiftness that it wasn't long before 19th century nerds were coming up with ways to make the game more efficient and less enjoyable. A few centuries later, here we are, standing in the ruins of what was once a confusingly proud institution dedicated to honoring baseball's best and/or consistently racist contributors.

In 1936, this building was finished, and some old hats and soiled relics were sealed behind glass. Fully grown adults would wander in, gaze at the unwashed loin cloth of an ancient slugger, and believe these violent, long-dead men were for some reason next-level humans. Of course, we know who the *real* next-level humans are: Our military's super-soldiers. If baseball critics thought performance-enhancing drugs were bad, imagine how they would have felt about the gene-hacked cyborgs currently defending us from a race of space-cockroaches, who were drawn to our planet's massive waste piles and oceans that are 90% garbage juice.

Ha ha, forgive me; I don't need to remind you all that there's a war going on, from which we are all trying to desperately distract ourselves through government-mandated fun, like this tour.

Anyway, this monument to a game invented in a shit-covered horse pasture or whatever stood for many decades and made a lot of people happy. But after the turn of the century, with corporate greed and rampant cheating having infiltrated the sport, this place became more like the National Hall of Pointless and Disingenuous Discourse. There was always a vein of desperate nostalgia flowing through it, fueling each generation as it reliably accused the next one of ruining the game. From that vein branched eye-rolling sanctimony, breathtaking pomposity, and—America's secret sauce—proud ignorance.

Sports writing in general was abandoned in the 2030s because Hall of Fame voters made the whole industry seem like a massive waste of time. Nowhere is that more evident than in this column here, one of the key representations of the moronic 2020s. It is a column in which a Hall of Fame voter consulted a neuroscientist for some reason to ask if his Hall of Fame voting habits, which included supporting an aggressive hatemonger, made him a bad person. It was a bizarre and widely mocked attempt to appear thoughtful on the topic of honoring horrible people. The article does not appear in the Hall to be commemorated, but rather, to be destroyed, as the last copy is housed here under the assumption that this structure, like countless others, will be decimated in a space-roach attack.

Most other records of ballots and the written discussions of their merit were classified by the government as "massively unessential." Of course, as we now know, after the "collection" phase of this initiative, the government never developed the part of the plan in which generations of human detritus were effectively and unharmfully disposed, leading to the massive buildup of waste that attracted the space-roaches...

Sorry. Sorry. I know. It's just, I can't stop thinking about it.

Sigh.

As we all know, 2020 was a cataclysmic year for most institutions, including baseball. The sport had big plans for that season in particular. It was to be Albert Pujols' 20th season. Yadier Molina was going to log his 2,000th hit. The league was going to honor *Field of Dreams*, a movie about a man so haunted by the spectre of his dead father that he stares into a corn field for an hour and a half until he realizes his daughter is choking on a hot dog. A game between the Yankees and White Sox would have been played on the field where the movie was filmed, but the game was canceled as part of a league wide "Everything is Canceled" policy.

There was also the Astros and Red Sox cheating scandal that was going to play a role in 2020. The game was teetering on the verge of a steroid-level scandal, only in this case, the syringes were "suspiciously positioned outfield cameras" and the performance-enhancer was "knowledge." This issue took over the sport as fans wondered why they even bothered watching a game so easily trivialized by the people playing it, and the Astros players demanded everyone just move on because it made them uncomfortable to talk about what they'd done.

But when the coronavirus blanketed America in early 2020, baseball came to a screeching halt like an equipment truck hauling a century of racism, labor disputes, and spitting. Baseball's biggest problems—the Astros' banging scheme, the possibility of other banging schemes, the ball suddenly becoming weightless—were put on hold so baseball's top minds could work out how it would survive in the pandemic.

For hundreds of years, baseball had existed outside reality, protected by a bubble of romanticization. Now, it appeared to be susceptible to all of the same politics and viruses that haunted the world around it. Fans were forced to consider: If this truly is America's Pastime, then perhaps it is a reflection of America's past times? And what does that mean for the future?

These were big, serious questions, and as usual, they were ignored in favor of small, loud arguments.

What was that?! Did you hear that?

Keep your voices down.

All they gave me for protection was this bat used to hit Mark McGwire's

70th home run in 1998, but I filled it with nails and I'm on stronger drugs than he was, so we may have an advantage if the space-roaches have gotten inside.

Oh, phew. It's just "Ballsy," MLB's last attempt at a mascot for the league! He was created for MLB to finally tap into the youth market in 2025. When he immediately failed to do so, the league gave up, called children "unreachable," and shuttered their marketing department.

Careful—I wouldn't try to take a picture with Ballsy. Or even get too close to him. I don't actually know who is in the suit right now, so I'm not sure how it's moving around.

Anyway, get together in a tighter formation, please, and we'll move on. And I just mean, stay away from the walls. Ironically, after all that talk about baseball's integrity in the early 2000s and late 2010s and early 2020s, the actual, structural integrity of this building is on the verge of collapsing.

Speaking of which, did you know that former baseball player Curt Schilling lived in the walls of our museum in protest for the last few years of his life, claiming it meant he had "gotten in"? He said that he "didn't need writers' permission" to pull himself through an access panel and scuttle about the duct system, living off rat meat and licking condensation off the walls. Giving an interview through an air vent, he said it was the "proudest moment of his legacy," and he would be correct.

Any questions? Yes, you there—wow, is that a baseball *cap?* You must be a true fan. What's that? You found it "in a literal sewer, near a pile of small bones?" Yikes.

Well, what's your question? "Where are all the baseballs?"

Well, actually, to our left here, we see a pile of baseballs. Just a big old mess of them. We tried giving them away to local leagues or fans—some of them have pretty rare signatures on them—but all the little league programs had been shut down, and eventually even the goat farm we were donating them to as food was like, "Please stop."

Sure, go ahead and sift through them. We'd just really devalued both baseball and handwriting by the end of the 2020s, so these have next to no worth, financially or culturally.

Hey, here's the room with all of Rob Manfred's rules in it. Manfred was a complicated man who never faced a league-wide problem he thought couldn't be solved by moving all the furniture around in his office. From cheating scandals to global health emergencies, he always knew baseball was one runner starting on second base in extra innings away from being completely fixed.

Unfortunately, "actual problems" weren't really his forte, making it difficult for fans to empathize with him. He may not have liked or understood the rules of baseball, but no one can claim he didn't have the fan experience at the fore-front of his thoughts day and night, as long as those fans were also billionaires and one of the owners of baseball's thirty franchises.

His new rules included, clocks between innings and pitching changes to speed the game up, filling the ball with something new every year just to see what would happen, like rusty nails, dead worms, and human teeth; forcing teams to use a spot on their 40-man roster for the mascot; and, in what was considered his only "actually good" rule, Mike Trout was to be rotated team-to-team throughout the league by way of an annual preseason raffle. To quote the commissioner's office, "No one wants to see Mike Trout play for the Angels, and since they're the Angels, no one will."

Well, that'll be all. On your way out, please take a coupon for half-priced corn cobs at Aubrey Huff's Mask-less Meat Pit across the street. All grown men weeping alone in a booth over wallet pictures of their families get a free appetizer.

Uh oh.

Yeah, I heard it too.

That klaxon blaring means another space-roach attack is imminent. Follow me down to the bunker that MLB used as a cloning lab in the final years of its existence. Don't worry, much like marketing baseball, they never quite figured out cloning, either. But if you hear someone begging for death, it'll either be the malformed Stan Musial that's still down there dragging its massive head on the floor through the darkened corridors, or me, quietly huddled in the corner with my hands over my ears.

This way!

(Don't) Take Me Out to the Ball Game (With Apologies to Norworth and Von Tilzer)

Ron Kaplan

Verse:
Twenty-twenty was baseball sad
We had corona and it was bad.
Was it too much to ask to go to the park, for a lark?
Finally in midsummer's heat
Came the news that we'd have our treat.
Sure, no fans were allowed in the seats
But we'll still get to watch while they play.

Chorus:
Don't take me out to the ballgame
I'll watch "The Show" on TV.
Who needs to pay for the snacks and beer?
Stay at home you'll have nothing to fear
From the folks who won't social distance
Or wear a mask the just the same
And it's one, two, three, three strikes you're out
Of the new ball game.

Verse:
Some will opt out, won't play at all
In the summer and through the fall.
Sixty games, a small sample size
For the prize, but that's wise.
The stats will be screwy, some will insist
They be acknowledged by asterisks.
They will ask if it's worth the risk
To have the game so watered down.

Repeat Chorus

Verse:
Players and owners both know the score;
Know just what they are fighting for.
Will the fans get to have their fun
In 2021?
Have to hope that no one succumbs
To the virus, that would be dumb.
Just the thought of it makes me numb
To see the sport crumble to dust.

Chorus

BASEBALL AS MY MUSE

Margie Lawrence

Having grown up blocks from the friendly confines of Wrigley Field, I had no choice but to fall in love with the Cubs.

The organ music and cheers of the crowd would drift through the open windows of my school, which sat a mere block from the bleacher entrance. And like many of my loves, the Cubs have disappointed me throughout my life but I still kept the hope alive that one day everything will be all right in the world and they – we - will win a World Series. 2016 was my epiphany and the religious experience fueled my artistic nature.

My first baseball memory involved 20 or so family members crowded around the portable TV cheering Sandy Koufax on during the 1963 World Series. Later on, I would pretend I was Sandy or Fergie Jenkins or Ken Holtzman, throwing what I perceived to be a curve ball at a small painted square on a brick wall. I was 11, it was 1969. My height was about that of a munchkin, and I may have weighed at 65 pounds. If only I could have played on a Little League team…but damn those girl chromosomes.

I spent close to 20 years involved in the theatre in Chicago and made a few excursions to the East Coast. In the mid 80's, I left the Windy City to travel and actually became a bigger fan than when I had been at home. Eventually I had to come back, and after a 12-hour car ride, I hit Wrigley on 8-8-88, the night that lights came to Wrigley.

It was an omen, since I was coming back home to attend the School of the Art Institute of Chicago (and the School of Baseball at Wrigley). Within the week I was once again basking in the sunshine of the bleachers and soaking up the sounds and smells of the ballpark: freshly mown grass, combined with grilled hot dogs, balls caught by leather gloves, and dorky organ music.

At school I drove my professors crazy with my "affliction" for baseball. My man was Ryno, #23, Ryne Sandberg, and no one could tell me different. 95% of my art was baseball-themed, but then again everyone at that point seemed to be a Cubs fan...we were contenders and the city was going nuts. I took my beat-up Ron Santo glove and scanned in the trim to make my first computer-generated piece and I have never looked back. After 24 years I have made more paintings and pencil renderings than computer pieces, but they all shine like a big "W" flag.

My subjects range from long-forgotten players like Chief Meyers up to the trio of Bryant, Rizzo and Russell in the dugout. I do prefer the old timers, as they all seem to have been such characters—Three Finger Brown, Cool Papa Bell, and Leo the Lip. When my buddy Ronny Santo passed away. I did the ugly cry in front of Wrigley and then the next year I did the happy ugly cry when he got into the Hall of Fame. But alas, there is more to baseball than my Cubbies.

I have also painted and sketched Satchel Paige, the oldest rookie, a beatific Joe D., and my hero, Jackie Roosevelt Robinson. Robert Feller's dad originated the Field of Dreams, building a park for his son, and I painted the family as "Baseball Gothic," an homage to Grant Wood. What did Durocher do besides manage Willie Mays? Well, he loved to scream at umpires. So I painted it.

The ideas poured out. An idealistic Josh Gibson dreaming of the Major Leagues. Ted Williams' smirk, which was almost as pretty as his swing. The iconic catch of Mays diminished against a wall of green. Ernie Banks, who still has the gold tooth he had when he played with the Kansas City Monarchs, and Hack Wilson's golden bat spraying RBIs all over the field. From Christy Mathewson to Monte Irvin to the greatest face in all of baseball, Casey Stengel, they are all in my portfolio.

Contributors

SABR BASEBALL CARDS COMMITTEE encourages more interactive knowledge sharing about the history and importance of baseball cards as a representation of the game itself. This research will help document the link between the baseball card industry and the game's popularity. Several members of the committee including Jason Schwartz, Paul Borelli, Mike Bryan Todd Clark, Chris Kamka, John Racanelli, Brian Mazmanian, Benjamin Sabin and Paul Ember have contributed their art to Turnstyle.

GABRIEL BOGART Gabriel Bogart is a writer, music aficionado, hot sauce chef, and rabid baseball fan from Seattle, WA. He learned to love baseball watching Ken Griffey, Jr. in person. Previously, Gabe's work has been featured in Corvus Review, Fahmidan Journal, a small run book of his own poetry titled "Will They Reminisce Over You?", and he posts baseball trivia at maxsporting-studio.com. If he were Commissioner of Major League Baseball, bat flips might be mandatory. You can find him at @Rev_Gabelicious on Twitter.

PAUL BORELLI is a self-taught visual artist living in Austin, Texas. He took up painting 15 years ago after retiring from a career as a technical writer in the computer industry. His work has been shown at several exhibits and places of business in the Austin area. His interest in baseball dates to 1967 when he began collecting baseball cards. He accepts occasional commissions and can be reached at beestguy@gmail.com for any inquiries about purchasing completed works.

JACK BUCK lives in Boise, Idaho. He is the author of the books Deer Michigan and Gathering View.

DICK BUTLER – is a retired attorney who still misses the exploding scoreboard at Comiskey Park.

RICHARD CAMPBELL is a Marketing Professor at Sonoma State University by day and an A's fan by night.

KALWINDER SINGH DHINDSA wrote: "Over the past two years I've written hundreds of poems every now and again I touch upon baseball one of my great life heroes is a man called Steve Bloomer. He played football and baseball in England. He was he was a real champion. I've written about him in my story "My father in the Last Legend of Pear Tree". There is a dream sequence at the end of it where I finally meet my hero as well as other figures and a nod to W.P. Kinsella (Shoeless Joe/ Field of Dreams). I also recently started collecting cigarette cards and have the odd baseball one or two in my collection. Some were sent to me for free from the US. I also make my own too. I wrote the Honu$ poem after Keith Oberman became a friend of mine and asked if I could make the Honus card speak... move his lips... which I did for him."

PETER M. GORDON is a long- time member of SABR (currently Central Florida Chapter) and contributed biographies to over 18 SABR books. He's published over 100 poems in various journals, along with two collections: Two Car Garage and Let's Play Two, Poems About Baseball. He won the Thomas Burnett Swann Poetry Prize from the Gwendolyn Brooks Writers Association of Central Florida. He's a member of the 19th Century and Deadball Committees. He teaches in Full Sail University's Film Production MFA program and lives in Orlando, Florida.

JOHN L. GREEN resides in Danville, CA. A member of the Lefty O'Doul Chapter since 1990, he grew up loving the Oakland Oakes, and when he was 7, he learned how to calculate a batting average. On that day, he became a life-long lover and fan of the game, stats, and history.

BRUCE HARRIS has been a SABR member since 2006. He has contributed to SABR's Biography Project and the Games Project. His article, "Baseball and Briar" appears in the 2007 Baseball Research Journal.

DAVID HOLDEN is a visual artist based in Toronto, Canada. He was educated at Queen's University (B.F.A. and York University (M.F.A.). David has exhibited his paintings at various galleries and art centres in Canada and the U.S. He creates representational paintings examining ideas of nostalgia. For the last few years, he has focused on the theme of baseball. David grew up in Montreal collecting baseball cards, playing on the local diamonds, cheering for the Expos and listening to his grandfather's stories of playing in the Montreal Independent Baseball league in the 1920s. David's work can be seen online at davidholden.com and on Instagram at davidholdenpainter.

RYAN ISAAC worked in baseball operations and scouting for 13 years, mostly with the San Diego Padres. He writes about his experiences in baseball at warningtrackpower.substack.com. Ryan lives in Carlsbad, Calif. with his wife and two children.

JOHN JAKICIC – Born April 23, 1950 in Chicago, White Sox fan and retired banker (Bank of America). Married 38 years (Christine) and going along happily. Previous writing experience – absolutely none. Greatest Accomplishment – Pee Wee League Batting Champ in 2nd grade (then found out I couldn't hit anything that curved). Saddest Childhood Moment – listening to a White Sox game on the radio in 1958 when Billy Pierce (my favorite White Sox player) lost a perfect game with one out to go versus the Washington Senators. Years later, I immediately understood what Bart Giamatti meant when he wrote that the game is designed to break your heart … with help from Ed Fitzgerald.

RON KAPLAN is the author of 501 Baseball Books Fans Must Read before They Die and Hank Greenberg in 1938: Hatred and Home Runs in the Shadow of War. His blog -- Ron Kaplan's Baseball Bookshelf is the longest-running site devoted to the literature and pop culture about the national pastime. His articles and reviews have appeared in such publications as Mental Floss, Baseball America, Irish America, American Book Review, and MultiCultural Review among many others.

DUANE VICTOR KEILSTRUP is Professor Emeritus at the University of Texas at Arlington and has been a SABR member for nearly 20 years. He has contributed a chapter in the SABR book The Team That Couldn't Hit: The 1972 Texas Rangers and an article in the second issue of the SABR Journal "Turnstyle." Dr. Keilstrup is Editor Emeritus of a scholarly journal and recently wrote The Christian Professor in the Secular University: Singing and Soaring in Paths of Joy. He also has a weekly program online devoted to vintage music and comedy shows form the golden age of radio. He is an avid fan of the Texas Rangers in Arlington, Texas where he and Glenda, his wife of 58 years, reside.

FRANCIS KINLAW has been a member of SABR since 1983. He resides in Greensboro, North Carolina and writes extensively about baseball, football, and college basketball. Although he has lived in the South for most of his life, he has been a life-long fan of the Detroit Tigers. Upon retiring in 20009 after more than three decades in local government, he thoroughly enjoyed visiting the Baseball Hall of Fame in Cooperstown with his wife, four sons, and other family members.

JUSTIN KLUGH is a writer living in Baltimore by way of Philadelphia. He has written for Baseball Prospectus, Fangraphs, SB Nation, and contributed to the last three Baseball Prospectus Annuals. His podcast, The Dirty Inning, looks back at the dumbest innings in Phillies history, and was listed as one of the best Philly podcasts of 2018.

ADAM KORENGOLD Adam Korengold, of Alexandria, Virginia, is a SABR member since 2020. A resident of the Washington, DC area for most of his life, he is a graduate of Walter Johnson High School, named for the Washington Senators great. He currently an Analytics Lead for the National Library of Medicine in Bethesda, Maryland.

Adam began making card paintings in acrylic on vintage baseball cards, dating from the 1960s to the 2020s, to bring new life to pieces which are more typically considered to be ephemera. He draws inspiration from Russian iconography, color field paintings, and other movements in art and design to create unique, playful, and elegant miniature paintings. It has been a much-loved way to pass the wintertime during the continuing pandemic.

MARGIE LAWRENCE is a nationally known fine artist that has a large inventory of baseball themed art. She has been using art to celebrate our national pastime. She has collected throughout the country and has representation in Chicago through Victor Armandariz. If there is ever have another issue dedicated to artists that use baseball as a muse, please consider her.

NORMAN L. MACHT is the author of more than 35 books, including the 3-volume biography of Connie Mack. His life span is equal to 75 per cent of the history of the American League.

PAUL MOOREHEAD is a fan of all the views of a baseball game: athletics, artistry, analytics, history. He is a mediocre middle-aged softball player, sometimes a shortstop, and has been a SABR member since 2005. This is his first published poem.

DONNA MUSCARELLA is a photographer and fourth-generation baseball enthusiast. She has a passion for combining those two loves, which in part led her to release her debut custom trading card set in 2021. The set combines Donna's photography of Hinchliffe Stadium with facts about its Negro Leagues ties and was featured in an article on the SABR Baseball Card Research Committee's Blog. It is Donna's hope that the cards will inspire others to learn more about Hinchliffe and the Negro Leagues. Produced in a limited edition of 50, the set is available for purchase with 20% of the revenue earmarked for donation to various organizations that preserve and promote Negro Leagues baseball history. Twitter and Instagram: @TheLensOfDonnaM. E-mail: TheLensOfDonnaM@gmail.com.

KYLE NEWMAN – KG Newman is a sportswriter who covers the Broncos and Rockies for The Denver Post. His first three collections of poems are available on Amazon. The Arizona State University alum is on Twitter @KyleNewmanDP and more info and writing can be found at kgnewman.com. He lives in Parker, Colorado, with his wife and two kids.

JOEY NICOLETTI is the author of five full-length poetry collections and four chapbooks, most recently, Boombox Serenade (BlazeVox, 2019) and Fan Mail, which is forthcoming from Broadstone Books later this year. He teaches creative writing at SUNY Buffalo State. He is a member of the Luke Easter Chapter.

MATT PERRY is a SABR member based in Arlington, MA and a graduate student studying writing at Salem State University. I have been previously published as part of the SABR Games Project and BioProject.

KENT PUTNAM Kent Putnam took up photography as a hobby as a young adult and made the transition from film to digital several years ago. His photographs have been selected for numerous local juried shows and have received many awards. His website can be found at https://fourstrongwindsphotography.zenfolio.com/. Kent is a member of the Florida Bar and is retired from employment with the State of Florida. He is recording secretary of the Buck O'Neil Chapter of SABR. Kent and his wife, Paula, and their cat Figaro make their home in Tallahassee.

JASON SCHWARTZ is co-chair of the SABR Baseball Cards Committee. Collecting cards was a hobby he began during the pandemic to raise money for charity by making "baseball card art" from the cards in his collection and various craft supplies.

KURT SINCLAIR wrote, the pandemic year of 2020, despite all of its challenges, turned out to be one of opportunity. Opportunity to make Lemonade out of Lemons. To help maintain some sense of sanity through all of its ups and downs, I sought refuge through my artwork. It often became a means of self-preservation. Through the long winter, spring, summer and fall of 2020, I luckily found that the game of baseball had not changed. Baseball, as I have always known, continued to provide exciting moments to appreciate and ultimately celebrate. For that, I am forever a fan.

GEORGE SKORNICKEL has been a die-hard Pirates fan for over sixty years. A retired educator, he is the author of "Beat'em Bucs: the 1960 Pittsburgh Pirates" and his articles have appeared in The Baseball Research Journal and The National Pastime. He is the president of the Forbes Field Chapter of SABR and has given presentations there on a variety of topics. He lives near Pittsburgh in Tarentum, PA with his wife Kathy and Lab Dexter.

JOSEPH STANTON is widely published as an art historian, literary historian, baseball historian, and poet. My poems and essays have appeared previously in Poetry, New Letters, Harvard Review, Antioch Review, Poetry East, New York Quarterly, Cortland Review, Sport Literate, Elysian Fields Quarterly, Spitball, Nine, Aethlon, Michigan Quarterly Review, American Art, Art Criticism, and many other magazines. I have published more than 700 poems in journals and anthologies. I have published six books of poems: Moving Pictures, Things Seen, Imaginary Museum, A Field Guide to the Wildlife of Suburban Oahu, Cardinal Points: Poems on St. Louis Cardinals Baseball, and What the Kite Thinks: A Linked Poem. My other sorts of books include Looking for Edward Gorey, The Important Books, Stan Musial: A Biography, and A Hawaii Anthology. I have frequently collaborated with visual artists, playwrights, composers, and other poets. My published essays include pieces on the history of baseball poetry, the history of baseball art, and the history of the St. Louis Cardinals.

BRYAN STEVERSON is a founding member of the East Tennessee chapter of SABR, a HOF and NLBM member. He is the author of two books: Amazing Baseball Heroes, Inspirational Negro League Stories published in 2011 and Baseball, A Special Gift from God in 2014.

JARED WYLLYS covers baseball for the Chicago Sun-Times and Forbes Sports. He lives in Wheaton, Illinois with his wife and four kids.

ADAM YOUNG grew up in Oklahoma and Mississippi, earned an MFA in English at the University of Mississippi, and teaches creative writing at Middle Georgia State University. 2018.

Turnstyle: The SABR Journal of Baseball Arts

Back Issues $9.95 paperback/$5.99 ebook

Turnstyle: Issue 1

The inaugural issue of Turnstyle in which "your eyes will behold the work of many SABR writers and artists who find inspiration in the romance, mythology, history, and discipline that baseball offers. We do not in any way intend to duplicate the great work of other literary baseball journals. Rather we embrace the legacy those journals have bequeathed to us; we are encouraged to continue what has been an integral part of baseball—the art and literature dedicated to the game." Included are Yakyu Haikus by Tetsuo Furukawa, the art of Cuban illustrator and artist Andez, and an interview with artist Andy Brown. Sprinkled throughout readers will be delighted to find cartoons and excerpts from 19th century newspapers and writing on baseball, including satire from Henry Guy Carleton, Hugh E. Keogh, and Marcus "Brick" Pomeroy. Includes contributions by Tom Lagasse, B. Craig Grafton, Bill Barna, George R. Skornickel, Andrea Long, W.B. (Bryan) Steverson, R.J. Lesch, Bob Brady, Edwin Epps, Matthew H. Schaedler.

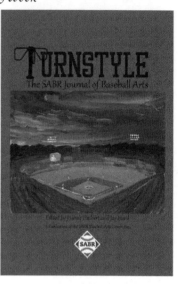

Turnstyle; Issue 2

Thirty-six pieces in all fill the pages of Issue 2, including a baker's dozen poems, a dozen articles and autobiographical essays, seven stories, and over a dozen paintings and illustrations. We have an exploration of the art of Joaquin Newman, an Oakland-based artist who combined the Mexican tradition of calaveras (skeleton paintings for Day of the Dead) with baseball cards for a series of paintings, one of which graces the issue's front cover. Andrea Long writes about how baseball connected her with her father, even after his passing, and George Skornickel looks back on a special Opening Day he shared with his mother when he was young. Several writers referenced the trying circumstances of the 2020 pandemic, including Bill Nowlin's closing essay about the unique wait for 2020 Opening Day. Anika Orrock brings us a lively, and true, story of a nun who played baseball, while three members of the Moonlight Graham Society recount how each of them made their sole appearance in a professional game, a la the society's namesake. In "Ninth Inning" writer Bradley Stribling gives us a fictionalized account of a real game: a 1925 match between a Negro League ball team and a Ku Klux Klan team, while Bryan Erwin sends us deep into the gut-churning moral dilemma of a player whose split-second decision on the field may have far-reaching consequences in "The Spoiler."

Made in the USA
Middletown, DE
29 January 2023